The Inventions of Louis Pouzin

Chantal Lebrument • Fabien Soyez

The Inventions
of Louis Pouzin

One of the Fathers of the Internet

Springer

Chantal Lebrument
Plourhan, France

Fabien Soyez
Paris, France

ISBN 978-3-030-34835-9   ISBN 978-3-030-34836-6   (eBook)
https://doi.org/10.1007/978-3-030-34836-6

The Work was first published in 2018 by Economica with the following title: "Louis Pouzin - l'un des Pères de l'Internet" (ISBN-13: 978-2717870473). All rights reserved.

This Springer imprint is published by the registered company Springer Nature Switzerland AG.
The registered company address is: Gewerbestrasse 11, 6330 Cham, Switzerland

Foreword

I was honored when the authors asked me to write a Foreword to the English edition of Louis Pouzin's biography. I first met Louis in the fall of 1975 at the Fourth Data Comm Symposium in Quebec City. We knew of Louis and the CYCLADES network before that. It was an impressive first encounter.

That may have been as close to a perfect symposium as a young grad student could attend. Perfect crisp fall days, in one of the most beautiful cities in North America at the new Hotel Concorde located just outside the city's wall. From my room on a high floor a panorama of the Plains of Abraham, the old city, the Chateau Frontenac, and the St Laurent! Breathtaking! What a great place to encourage discussion! And we had a lot we wanted to talk about. For the small group of researchers, networking was an incredibly exciting topic that had captured the imagination.

The program was an interesting amalgam of the traditional topics in data communication and the exciting new packet switching research. Robert Fano, from Project MAC, gave the keynote. I remember him saying that they had built the first timesharing system to make more efficient use of the hardware but found that the collaboration it enabled was far more important. He expected that we would find that networks were very similar. I remember thinking that he was undoubtedly right, and we were already beginning to see that. (Although, in our enthusiasm, we failed to anticipate the dark side of "collaboration" we are plagued with today.) There was such interest in networking that the leading researchers were in great demand: Larry Roberts, Vint Cerf, Bob Kahn, Donald Davies, André Danthine, Derek Barber, Louis Pouzin, and others were going from conference to conference to talk about networking. They jokingly referred to it as the "Network Traveling Circus."

Today, it is hard to communicate just how small the computing field was, and networking was a much smaller part of that.

But the star of the meeting was definitely Pouzin. He was everywhere, giving a lecture, leading a discussion (even if not officially), arranging a fine dinner every evening for the core of the group. One evening dinner was a little earlier than civilized so we could be back for evening sessions. But Louis had us well-organized: With precisely the right number of taxis outside the hotel at the appointed hour, off we went! We would troop into the restaurant, settle into 3 or 4 big tables, somehow order dinner around the ongoing discussion of what we had heard that day, or what someone was working on or planning as we tried to figure out this networking tiger we had by the tail (or it had us), pausing to notice that this was an outstanding restaurant; we were just winding down from a wonderful dessert, when Louis would suddenly appear, announcing it was time to go. (Timing is everything!) Taxis were waiting outside. We piled in again, to head back for the evening "birds of a feather" sessions!

This is especially vivid for me, because it didn't end so simply. We happened to pile Louis' cab with either the craziest or most competent driver in Quebec. Louis must have told them time was of the essence. Our cabbie was whipping through the narrow streets of the old city shifting frantically at every turn, then speeding out the Grande Allée, through the old wall of the city at high speed. Ahead of us was a red light, the driver momentarily let up on the gas, clearly to take his place in the line of cars waiting for the light. *NO!!* it must have been to assess the situation, because he tromped on the gas again as he pulled into the left lane *(wha!)* and headed right for the oncoming traffic! *(OMG! We are about to die!)* At the last possible second, the light turned green and at precisely that instant, we turned left! With us howling with laughter!

It was no different 35 years later, when we all happened to be in Brussels. Louis had suggested that our organizer call a particular restaurant near our hotel and make a reservation for the group. He called to make the reservation for 12 and was told the restaurant did not take reservations. Perplexed "so sorry," wondering what to do next, he thought aloud, "M. Pouzin told me you did." "O, *Louis!!*," came the reply, "your table will be ready." And it was. I was left wondering Louis doesn't live in Brussels; he lives in Paris! How many restaurants in other parts of the world, would there be the same reaction!?

That was the beginning of what became nearly a half century of working with Louis and his guys! It was immediately clear that Louis was one of those rare combinations of brilliant, charismatic leaders who could build a tight dedicated team and give them their head and great things would happen. What they were doing had that intuitive feel that it was "right." The pieces fit together well, there were exciting new directions, and we could see that the issues we hadn't gotten to considering in detail would likely fall in place quite nicely.

Before going too much further, I have to make an admission. I wasn't really working *with* Pouzin all that much in those early days. I was too far down the totem pole for that! Louis was one of the august leaders of networking that hobnobbed with the powers that be. Me, I was just learning! But Louis's guys were my age and we worked with them a lot. They were not only very smart but great companions after work. Everyone worked hard and played hard. It was later that Louis and I began to spend more time working together and found we had just as much in common as I had with his guys.

Why were we even *at* the Fourth Data Communication? We were on another ARPA project at the University of Illinois in Urbana-Champaign building the first "massively" parallel computer, ILLIAC IV. ILLIAC IV was an array processor of 64 processors (originally planned to be 256). Sounds pretty small by today's standards, but it was a huge undertaking in 1968. I had joined the operating system group in 1969. We were given the task of putting our site on the ARPANET. From a distributed systems point of view, networking was clearly a lot more interesting than an array processor. Many of us saw networking as more a distributed computing problem than a telecom problem. But that wasn't the only reason.

The world all of this lived in was quite different from today. I said that the worldwide networking community was small. The computer industry itself wasn't that big. Many universities had yet to form computer science departments. That doesn't mean the world was like today only with fewer in the field. It was a time of intense creativity in virtually all fields. As indicated recently by all of 50th anniversaries there have been (or are about to be) in 2018, 2019, 2020. The Beatles, the Stones, Zappa, and many others, the ARPANET, Engelbart's NLS and the invention of the mouse, the Apollo moon landing, Woodstock, John Cage, Sesame Street, etc. And it wasn't just technology and the arts. It was also politics and civil unrest: the anti-nuclear demonstrations in Europe and the USA, May 1968 in France, anti-Vietnam War demonstrations, civil rights, Earth Day, assassinations of JFK, RFK, and MLKing, kidnappings (Hearst), the movies "Z" and "Medium Cool," Chicago 68 Democratic Convention, Kent State, etc.

If you had started grad school before the mid-1960s, it was more likely you could avoid the social unrest and only saw it on the news. If you were an undergraduate at the time, there was a better chance of getting wrapped up in it. And if you were working on the largest DoD project on campus, it was unavoidable. In those days, you could tell hardware guys from software guys by looking at them. Once four of us from the Illiac IV OS team were on our way to Philadelphia where Illiac was being built. As we were changing planes in Chicago, the young flight attendant said with a touch of expectant awe, "Are you guys in a band!?" I replied, "No, we're crypto-fascist lackeys of the military-industrial complex." ;-) The phrase campus radicals had tagged us with. We were probably more radical than they were. A poster of Chairman Mao hung in our machine room. It was a time of intense social unrest both in the USA and Europe. We were the target of demonstrations and we participated. There was an attempted firebombing of our office. We were getting an education in computer science, political science, and the politics of big science all at once. (At first, the radicals claimed that the Project had been secretly approved. When we proved that wrong, they shifted to "we don't think classified research should be done on campus!" To which we said, "We agree! And it can't be." Unrelated cost overruns were creating political problems with ARPA. The campus unrest provided a handy excuse to solve that problem as well, which ended with IlliacIV going to Mountain View where it could do classified research. A much longer story.) When I look back on all that happened in a very short period of time, it is stunning. They were heady times. Times that Louis was born for! As the reader will find, these kinds of events were affecting Louis and his guys as well.

Louis Pouzin had worked on Project MAC at MIT where he had invented the shell and established himself as one of the "new breed" of bright young innovators in computing. Soon after the ARPANET came online, Pouzin returned to the States to look it over. The ARPANET had been built to lower the cost of research on other ARPA projects by allowing sites to share resources. BBN had done a good job. In fact, I have often said BBN got too much right the first time! There was not much of anything that *had* to be fixed immediately that would also create the opportunity to take the next step. The ARPANET quickly became a necessity for us. But the ARPANET was a production network from the start. BBN had one 2 hour period a week for experimentation and new software releases. It was not a research network and there was a lot we didn't know about networking. Louis resolved to build a packet network in France. This is where Louis's talent really shone: His ability to assemble and build a tight team of brilliant engineers who knew how to tackle a problem from scratch. Yes, I just mentioned this, but it is hard to say it is enough. I have worked with a lot of groups, but there has never been a group that just seemed to click like these guys did.

Of course, they didn't want to simply copy what ARPA had done; instead, they would build a network to do research on networks. To do that they proceeded as any good researcher would: they set out to build a network that made as few assumptions as possible about how networks should work and was structured to facilitate experimentation. They got help from BBN personnel so that, as Dave Walden aptly put it, "they wouldn't make the same mistakes we did!"

As any systems designer knows, with a complex project that has never been done before, regardless of how much design and forethought has gone into it, once there is an implementation, one can see improvements or sometimes major design strategies that would be much better. The advantage Pouzin and the CYCLADES team had was the opportunity to think through the problem given the ARPANET experience with an eye to where it was going to have to go. They weren't just trying to solve the immediate problem, but to design for a point in the future. Also, if this was to be a network to do research on networks, they wanted to challenge every traditional assumption: Is this really necessary? What would happen if it were relaxed? As they went through the process, several new concepts emerged.

Louis and his team quickly made two major insights: First was the *datagram*, as the minimal assumptions about what a packet should be. Traditional networks had been tied to circuits, paths, both by the technology and by the fact that voice was continuous. But data was bursty, it was naturally in packets. To some extent, packet switching was obvious. The problem is passing data between computers. Data is stored in buffers in a computer. So, pick up a buffer and send it! Relay the buffer (now a packet). To do anything else would be a lot more work! What would happen if that were leveraged? What properties did a packet have to have?

They could use datagrams as a tool to understand the internal workings of the network itself and what if anything else is needed. Why assume that every packet had to follow the same path. Why did resources have to be allocated for the path when it was created? Operating systems had shown that dynamic, statistical resource allocation was several orders of magnitude more efficient. Networks could use that. The *datagram* is a packet whose delivery is not guaranteed, and its routing through the network is independent of any other datagrams sent before or after. Datagrams move through the network independently, not necessarily tied to a fixed path.

Experimentation would likely require replacing protocols. To do this easily, "black boxes" (layers) were needed, so it could be done without changing the interface. This would provide the flexibility for new developments as new discoveries were made. This uncovered two major differences between traditional networks and computer networks: In traditional networks, the end devices were merely *attached* to the networks, while in computer networks, the end devices *participated* in the network, and as noted above traffic was much more dynamic, more stochastic. In addition, it was noted that different layers did not all terminate in the same systems. The layers consisted of collections of cooperating entities at different scopes, which increased with increasing *rank*. These were critically important insights.

CYCLADES wasn't the first to adopt layers as an organizing principle. In 1968, Edgar Dykstra had published his landmark paper on the the operating system that proposed that layers could be used to organize an OS. Each layer performed a function and provided a service to the layer above. Dykstra conjectured that once a function was done, there was no need to repeat it in the layers above. Not surprisingly, layers had been quickly picked up in the ARPANET in 1968 to organize the host software. The problem of connecting computers to the ARPANET switches (called IMPs) was an OS problem. (It is interesting to note that the layers were not used in the design of the IMP subnet). It was the host software that brought layers to networking. Being OS programmers, it was natural that they should model the work after an operating system. The first thing they needed was some sort of interprocess communication (IPC) on which to build the resource-sharing applications. For this, they created the Host–Host Protocol. They also created the application protocols for basic resource sharing. It was a common view. Dykstra's concept of layers seemed a perfect fit for this problem. Since they saw the resource-sharing network in terms of operating systems, it was natural that they found that layers made sense here as well:

Applications (Telnet, FTP, RJE; basic OS functions)
Host-to-host (NCP; interprocess communication)
IMP-to-host (the network device driver)
The physical wire

The CYCLADES team then had the opportunity to apply layers to the whole system: the hosts and the switches. This gave us the traditional layers we are all familiar with:

Application layer
Transport layer
Network layer
Data link layer
Physical layer

Furthermore, Pouzin reasoned that no matter how much effort was put into making the network perfectly reliable, the hosts would not trust the network to be reliable and would check to ensure nothing was lost. Conversely, he also understood that, at some point, there would be diminishing returns for the network to put effort into reliability. It would be more efficient for the hosts to handle them, since the hosts were looking for errors anyway. If the network only made a "*best effort*" and let the hosts do the recovery, this would not adversely impact performance, but the network could be less complex, more efficient, and cheaper to build. It would facilitate dynamic resource allocation, which would improve performance while also being much more resilient to failures. *CYCLADES originated the idea of the "best effort" datagram service, with an end-to-end transport protocol in the hosts to ensure reliability.*

To fully understand the contribution of Pouzin and the CYCLADES team, the rationale behind these layers needs some explanation. The data link layer was a point-to-point protocol, very close to HDLC, to detect and recover corrupted packets by retransmission. (This was also true for the ARPANET.) An HDLC-like protocol would be reliable between the store and forward switches, or routers. (The term "router" was not in use yet. At the time if they were called anything, they were called switches. Since the term "switch" has often been used for devices that switch in the physical layer, we will use the term "router" to emphasize that the relaying was done in software. Of course, today routers do the network layer in the hardware.) Louis and the CYCLADES team understood that transport primarily recovered from loss due to congestion and the rare memory errors during relaying. Papers from 1972 recognize congestion as an issue and a natural part of the CYCLADES research program. CYCLADES project members had begun investigating congestion in networking in general as well as datagram networks in particular. Over the next 10 years or so, many other researchers were also looking at the congestion problem in both connection and connectionless networks to minimize the probability of loss. It would be nearly 15 years before the Internet even realized congestion could occur.

Hence, we can summarize the lower four layers as worked out by the CYCLADES team as follows:

Physical layer provides the "wires."

Data link layer has small scope and provides sufficient error control to ensure that end-to-end error control is cost-effective.

Network layer has a wider scope and does relaying and routing, but with datagrams is susceptible to congestion, requiring packets to be discarded.

Transport layer has the same scope as the network layer and provides end-to-end error control ensuring a reliable data stream to the application, recovering packets lost in the network layer or has occurred outside the data link layer during relaying. It is the transport layer that creates a reliable communication using an unreliable network.

CYCLADES' contribution wasn't just the existence of an end-to-end transport protocol to the design of the protocol itself. Up until this time, data transfer protocols had a fixed "window" for flow control. This led to additional complexity: If the user did not or could not take the newly arrived data, two additional protocol commands were required. CYCLADES solved these problems by allowing the size of the window to vary by sending credit of how many packets can be sent with the acknowledgment. Not only does this allow the flow to quickly respond to changes in the availability of buffers but eliminates the need for the additional commands.

CYCLADES also introduced the distinction between the letter (or service data unit, SDU) and the protocol message size (or protocol data unit, PDU). This gave the protocol the flexibility to take an amount of data significant to the user and either fragment it or concatenate it with other data into sizes convenient to the transmission characteristics but retain the ability to deliver the original unit of data to the remote user. Making it easy for both the application and the transport protocol. *These have served as the basis of virtually all modern transport protocols.* The only thing missing from CYCLADES TS that was later incorporated into its successor, OSI TP4, was Richard Watson's seminal result in 1980 that the necessary and sufficient condition for synchronization for reliable data transfer is to enforce an upper bound on three times: maximum packet lifetime, maximum time before an Ack is sent, and maximum time to exhaust retries. Incorporating Watson's result not only improves the robustness of the protocol but also the security. TCP does not have the letter or SDU concept, nor does it incorporate Watson's discovery.

In addition, CYCLADES got the addressing structure correct. Recognizing that addresses named the entity in the layer that processed the protocol. For the CYCLADES network, this meant that there were application names, network addresses, and if necessary, data link addresses. Later when CYCLADES considered the problem of internetworking, this required only a slight change with addresses added to an Internet transport layer. The CYCLADES model for internetworking consisted of location-independent Application-names of global scope, location-dependent and route-independent Internet addresses of global scope, location-dependent and route-independent network addresses of (smaller) scope of the individual networks, and data link addresses over the scope of the multi-access media. The research community adopted this approach in the mid-1970s by adding an overlay Internet layer. This avoids the n × n translation problem that confronted the PTTs (and still does) by making it an n × 1 problem. By 1983, the Internet had lost this overlay in favor of protocol translation at the boundaries as the PTTs had done. In this approach, either for a network or an Internet, multihoming is inherently supported, and although CYCLADES did not get this far, mobility is supported with no additional protocols. The Internet has yet to find a solution to multi-homing, and the proposals for mobility require additional complex protocols and are overly complex.

But far more important than all of these important new insights into networking:

What Pouzin and his team were pursuing wasn't just datagrams with an end-to-end transport but a whole new paradigm of networking. This is generally unrecognized. A few years ago, when two MIT professors suggested data-grams and transport were just the two new things added to the traditional view of networking, I was so taken aback that I stammered to reply that "no, it was a whole new paradigm" and thinking "OMG, you didn't know?" We knew that the devotees of virtual circuits certainly didn't, but we assumed that the advocates of datagrams did! I am convinced that there was much about this model that the CYCLADES team knew, suspected but hadn't yet written down, or assumed were obvious and didn't need to be explicitly stated (such as the importance of the different scope of the layers). This new paradigm for networking had four primary characteristics:

1. It was a *peer network* of communicating equals not a hierarchical network connecting a mainframe master with terminals merely attached to the net-work but participating in the network.
2. The approach required coordinating *distributed shared state at different scopes*, which were treated as black boxes. This led to the concept of layers being adopted and generalized from operating systems.
3. There was a shift at this time from largely deterministic to *non-deterministic* designs, not just with datagrams in networks, but also with interrupt-driven, as opposed to polled, operating systems, and physical media like Ethernet, and the much greater efficiency of dynamic resource allocation
4. This was a computing model, *a distributed computing model*, not a telecom or datacom model. The network was part of the infrastructure of a distrib-uted computing facility.

This was a radical departure from what had existed before. The traditional ITU architecture for PTT and carrier networks was what I have called "beads-on-a-string." In this model, boxes and the wires connecting them are of pri-mary importance. Layers are merely modules. In the world of ITU, interfaces, the "wires" between boxes, are standardized. Furthermore, the PTTs argued that their networks were reliable (they weren't) and a transport layer was unnecessary. They had a major reason for making this argument. They wanted to put value-added services "in the network." What today one would call the "cloud." With the PTTs beads-on-a-string model, offering those services "in the network" implied they were within their monopoly. Only they could offer them. Worse, without something like the Carterphone decision in Europe, potentially the PTTs could say that the only computers that could be attached to their network were theirs, just as the only phones that could be connected had to be theirs.

Louis saw this coming and began to advocate for a more open network and against the PTTs. This was politically unwise, but it was true. Louis was a master of the presentation with his hand-drawn foils (no PowerPoint back then). In the book, one will read the author's and Louis's account of the ICCC meeting in 1976 in Toronto where all of this came to a head. Let me provide two other points of view of the same presentation. I was there and so was Mike O'Dell, then a young engineer, today a respected sage of the Internet.

Louis's talk was part of the early afternoon session in a huge ballroom at the Royal York Hotel. The other speakers had been running over their time and Louis was the last one. The night before, he had prepared his usual foils that included a castle labeled "PTT" with a user hanging from gallows from one of the parapets!;-) He was definitely on a roll and playing to the audience. Finding very entertaining ways to present the threat posed by the monopolies. The session was running late. People were filtering in and taking what few seats were left or standing along the wall. No one was leaving. The moderator stopped Louis and said, "Louis, we are running over our time." Louis replied, "What would you like me to do?" Never in a conference before or since have I heard the crowd spontaneously shout "Go on! Go on!" Louis finished his talk, while the PTT people in the front row furiously scribbled notes.

Andrew Russell, when writing his book *Open Standards and the Digital Age*, found O'Dell had been there as well. When O'Dell didn't reach Russell on the first try, he dashed off an email to me. Louis's charisma and ability to inspire were legendary, but one would expect that enthusiasm would cool over three decades.

This was O'Dell's reply in November 2012:

Hot diggity damn!
    I just tried calling Andrew Russell back and left voicemail.
    Yes indeedy—getting' to retell how I came to see the One True PACKET!
    "The First Powerhouse Church of the Presumptuous Assumption of The Blinding Light!"
    It was somewhere between a deep-south summer-steam-heat sweat-fest Full-Duplex Gospel Tent Revival and The Beatles on Ed Sullivan.

It don't get like that at Technical Meeting's, 'specially those infested with the acolytes of the Bell-shaped Idol. But when the DATAGRAMS Began To FLOW!

Lordy have mercy on your receive window! We wuz drinkin' from the FIRE HOSE OF TRUTH!

You could see it in the eyes of the idolaters—FEAR! I say FEAR of the DATAGRAM was upon them! They realized that they wuz in the midst of an epiphany—AN EPIPHANY, and SOMETHING DIED! The CIRCUIT as the atomic abstraction had been STRUCK DOWN by a MIGHTY BLAST of INSIGHT and the smokin' ruin just lay there on the floor, the unmistakable odor of lost hegemony stinkin' up the place.

SOULS WERE SAVED THAT DAY from a life of unceasing DIAL TONE!

The MIGHTY POUZIN finally bid the crowd disperse, but the fire lit that day in fact, changed lives.

For which I'm eternally grateful.

Neither the PTT monopolies nor the IBM's near monopoly met this new paradigm with great favor. It was a direct threat to their business models. With this new model, processes and layers are primary. Layers are seen as distributed processes cooperating to provide interprocess communication (IPC). They are a distributed resource allocator. Boxes are merely containers for the processes. All computing is at the edge, none can be "in the network".

The transport layer was a major threat. The end-to-end nature of the transport layer seals off the network relegating the carriers (the PTTs) to a commodity business. No one likes a commodity business. The margins are too narrow. Worse, the PTTs would lose a claim of monopoly on the lucrative value-added market.

It worked out as Louis predicted, but it wasn't the PTTs that benefited from services "in the network" but the Googles, Amazons, Facebooks, etc., and now 5G. And it wasn't the PTTs and IBM that thwarted the new paradigm although they weakened it, that was left for the Internet to do.

The Internet adopted datagrams and end-to-end transport with all of the zeal of the convert. All through the 1980s, they pushed everything to be connectionless whether it should be or not. It received knowledge on stone tablets. Not a research tool for better understanding dynamic stochastic resource allocation. TCP did not support the flexibility provided by the CYCLADES protocol. When IP was separated from TCP, they lost any pretense of an Internet layer and adopted the ITU model doing protocol translation at the boundary between networks (which doesn't work and requires a patch called Path MTU Discovery). They never extended or fixed their addressing model, so that multihoming and mobility are considerably more complex and inefficient. Through the 1980s, the Internet became a craft tradition. Once concepts become stone tablets (ceased to be challenged), all that is left is craft. By the turn of the twenty-first century, the Internet is at a dead end with the failure of the Future Internet effort and the complete adoption of the ITU model complete with control and data planes from ISDN and ATM. The Internet had stagnated by the early 1980s. If it were an OS, it would have been DOS. Whereas CYCLADES was well on its way to be the "UNIX of networking." So why did the Internet succeed? From the beginning the DoD was spending orders of magnitude more money on it than all of the corporate and NSF research combined, and even then, it was chump change in the DoD budget. Since it was taxpayers' money, they could then just give it away for free. The price was right. The meddling of big government gave us a flawed network, where there are strong indications that business left alone would have done far better.

In the mid-1990s, I decided I needed to find out what it was I really knew about networks. I had been spending so much time as the chair of one committee or another, where I had to present the committee's view not my own, I needed to find out what the fundamentals really were independent of technology, politics, or what existed.

Every operating system textbook talks about the separation of mechanism and policy; e.g., switching processes is mechanism and common, deciding what process to run next is policy, etc. But it never comes up in networking texts, even though it clearly exists. I wanted to apply it to protocols like CYCLADES, TS, TCP, TP4, etc., just to see what would happen and very interesting things did happen. I found that the protocol naturally cleaved into two parts that barely interacted and that by changing policy and applying the concept of abstract syntax, there was only one data transfer protocol with different policy sets. This led to seeing that the functionality of the layers repeated over different scopes.

On the surface, this appears to contradict Dykstra. It doesn't really. Functions do not repeat over the same scope. Also, it was apparent that there were more layers. Once one considers separating mechanism and policy, one can see that by not doing it, we had in effect been saying that there was one point in a 6- or 8-dimensional space (the number of mechanisms) that would work effectively over several orders of magnitude of performance. Absurd! No one would expect to see that. What we find is that *A layer is a distributed resource allocator supporting IPC over a given range of data rate, QoS, and scale.* Following this pattern and others and their implications, a much simpler model emerged. This was a huge complexity collapse, and problems that were currently requiring complex solutions simply disappeared. A short list of what we found was:

* Networking IPC and only IPC.
* A layer is a distributed application that does IPC.
* This leads to a layer being a specialization of a distributed application.
* Which leads to a unified model of applications, distributed applications, operating system.
* All layers have the same functions, a single layer that repeats.
* Connectionless is maximal shared state, not minimal.
* There is only one data transfer protocol and only one application protocol.
* Networking is defined by whether maximum packet lifetime is bounded. If not, then it is merely a file transfer, remote storage.
* There is no requirement for a global address space, or a global name space. IPv6 has been a waste of time.. . twice.
* Multihoming and mobility are a consequence of the structure, i.e., free, which also reduces router table size by a factor of at least 4 or 5.
* A layer (or network) can be renumbered in seconds without the loss of data. Actually, two layers can be renumbered at the same time without losing data.
* The resulting structure is inherently more secure, without NATs or firewalls.

The work to implement and productize this model is called RINA; more information can be found at www.pouzinsociety.org.

At the same time, I started digging into the history of networking to understand how we had gotten to where we were. I became convinced that patterns I was picking up were from where CYCLADES had left off. If CYCLADES had not been shut down, we would have had these insights much sooner. Now Louis is devoting much of his time to promoting RINA. The difference was neither of us was looking for something that works. We had been trying to find out what the problem told us. Do what the problem says. Charles Kettering said, "A problem well-defined is a problem half-solved." He was right.

Louis Pouzin has made a big difference in our world. My regret is that he and his ability to inspire and excite, his insights, and his ability to build teams could have had so much more impact. The question when he started was, "Can France (or Europe) innovate?" Could they have created the Internet? Could they create the next "big thing"? They had it in their hands. In fact what they had was far superior to the Internet we ended up with. It is important that original innovators are able to explore the insights more fully.

They needed the chance to run with it. They didn't get that chance.

Clearly the talent, the brains, the creativity is there. Louis and his team proved *that* as have others since. But the bureaucrats of innovation are not innovative. They are too tied to the status quo. They don't seem to understand that any big great new innovation is by its very nature going to skewer some sacred cows. The stress on "industry partners" is absurd. Consider the following scenario, go to a major industry and say: "we have these brilliant new insights and if we are right, it will invalidate your current business model, but triple your revenue." Would you give them money? Absurd! Never happen. How many industry partners did the ARPANET have? None! In fact, when the ARPANET was shown to AT&T they laugh at it. It was 20 years before they grudgingly showed some interest. New concepts take time; they have to skewer sacred cows; otherwise they won't have the impact. Early industry partners are the best way I know to squelch innovation. Louis Pouzin showed us that.

But it is almost 50 years later, we are smarter now, aren't we!? No, it appears that we haven't learned a thing. Louis is showing us that too.

Kinmundy, IL, USA   John Day

Preface

This book recounts the adventures of a man who, from scratch, invented one of the core elements for transmitting data over today's Internet, the datagram. He also created one of the most widely used computer programming languages, the Shell, and is currently, at age 88, a leader in the development of a new Internet, RINA.

Louis Pouzin is not well known in his own country, France, but is acclaimed by his peers internationally. He is a modest man, thinking only of the future and his next project, and is always very surprised when he receives a new distinction or award. He was pushed around, vilified, and ignored in France for years, but has not become bitter or anxious for recognition. And yet how many French scientists have met Queen Elizabeth II three times?

This lack of appreciation on the part of the French public is also due to the fact that, despite the motto "publish or perish" current in scientific circles, Louis has an impressive list of scientific publications but only one book, in English, to present his incredible achievement carried out with an exceptional team: the Cyclades project.

A Book for the Record

This book retraces this Cyclades epic, spearheaded by the best and brightest of French researchers, handpicked by Louis Pouzin for their intelligence and adaptability. It is also a saga of the 1960s at the legendary Massachusetts Institute of Technology (MIT) in Cambridge, where Louis Pouzin invented the Shell Multics scripts with his accomplice Glenda Schroeder, under the leadership of Professor Corbató. Louis and his team further developed the first French weather forecasting software, used for 15 years by *Météo France*; it also tells the story of the birth of what is now the Internet, thanks to the iron-strong will of a man who never doubts and has an amazing knack for surrounding himself with remarkable people.

Furthermore, although this period is now a well-recorded part of history, there are multiple web articles, videos, and transcripts of interviews with him; until now there was no published biography of Louis Pouzin.

Thus, this book is the story of a life and a team. It is the journey of a visionary intellectual who has always been one step ahead and has fully adapted to the twenty-first century though born into a very modest family in a small village in central France at the beginning of the twentieth century...

What makes Louis Pouzin so special is that he is a born leader and decision-maker who knows how to attract the right people to get projects done. He never admits defeat, even when shortsighted politicians absurdly order him to scrap his breakthroughs.

His project is our future: to have an independent and secure Internet.

Why Such a Book?

Another reason why it was so important to tell the story of the era surrounding the birth of the Internet is the fact that, with just a few exceptions, all the actors of this epic are still alive. Many are enjoying a peaceful retirement, but others are still very active, having led rich professional lives since the Cyclades years.

It is also an opportunity to tell the true story of the birth of the Internet... which has its roots in Europe, and not only, as some persistent legends would have it, in the USA. The datagram is French, and the Internet could also have been French, if it weren't for the incursion of vested interests in national politics.

This book puts into perspective the 50 years that have changed the world. If Louis Pouzin had not published his work after the end of Cyclades, it is likely that another researcher would one day have invented such a network... But would it have been open, interoperable, and simple?

Methodology

In its making, this book has strictly respected the basic rules of any journalistic investigation: interviews with those who made history, cross-referencing of sources, documentary research, etc.

Although Louis Pouzin has read some passages of this book, he decided to place his full trust in the authors to transcribe the highlights of his career and that of his whole team.

Authors with Direct Access to Sources

The authors' personal journeys have led them to cross the path of this story:

Fabien Soyez, 33 years old, is a journalist for Courrier Cadres, Socialter, CNET France, ZDNet, and Ulyces.co. Specialized in new technologies, the economy, and social innovation, he has been writing for 10 years on digital culture. He wrote the portrait of Louis Pouzin in 2016 for Ulyces... which he continued with this book.

Chantal Lebrument, 66 years old, discovered the Internet from its very beginnings in France in 1989. She participated in the early meetings on the Internet, which were still very confidential in the 1990s, and in the Journées d'Autrans near Grenoble from 1996 to 2009, dedicated to Internet use. With her scientific background, she participated in the adventure of the daily newspaper *Libération* from the 1970s to the 1990s and knows the requirements of writing a daily newspaper. Then, after moving into industry, she became an Internet specialist in multinational groups with a passion for domain names.

Since the late 1990s, she began following the saga of Internet governance, which is how she met Louis Pouzin with whom she now forms an inseparable pair. President of the Eurolinc association dedicated to natural languages on the Internet, she accompanies Louis on his many travels, a good manager of an unmanageable man.

This improbable combination, a true Dolby stereo of network history, allows for the cross-fertilization of a story that spans an entire century.

In other words, it was high time to devote a few pages to Mr. Louis POUZIN.

Plourhan, France   Chantal Lebrument
Paris, France   Fabien Soyez

Acknowledgments

Thank you, Margaret DUNHAM, for your essential role as copy editor in this adventure; we were familiar with your qualities as conference interpreter having availed ourselves of them often; the quality of this book's translation gives it wings to escape the borders of language.

This book would not have existed without the determination of General Marc WATIN-AUGOUARD, Founder and Delegate of the FIC for the Gendarmerie Nationale, who supported Louis Pouzin's work from the very beginning. But it is our French publisher, Jean PAVLEVSKI, founder and director of ECONOMICA Publishing, who has made it a reality. Thank you Jean for your kindness. I would also like to add the precious role played by our legal counsel, Isabelle LANDREAU; thank you for your loyalty and your judicious advice.

This list would not be complete without adding the members of EUROLINC, stalwart companions in the darkest years; Louis Pouzin has always been able to count on your unfailing friendship.

Thanks to the entire Cyclades team, and MICHEL GIEN in particular, for their help and advice during the almost historical investigation into the period 1960–1975. Many thanks also to MARC WEBER of the Computer History Museum (CHM) in Mountain View, who provided access to their numerous archives and oral interviews with the main protagonists in the history of the Internet and the web. This list would not be complete without mentioning John Day, tireless hero of the networks whose founding texts are the basis of the projects that are the focus of Louis Pouzin's work. A fair return of the things this book tries to explain.

Thanks also to the two network and computer historians PIERRE-ERIC MOUNIER-KUHN and VALERIE SCHAFER. This biography owes much to their detailed analysis and research.

Finally, thanks to Louis Pouzin's children for their kind support during this wonderful adventure.

Contents

1

Louis Pouzin's Youth (1931–1952)

All truth passes through three stages. First, it is ridiculed. Second, it is violently opposed. Third, it is accepted as being self-evident.
Arthur Schopenhauer (1788–1860)

1.1 Childhood

Once upon a time there was a bright and clever child who had an atypical education within a modest family in central France, in the Nièvre Department. A solitary family living in a single room at the father's sawmill, far from the village. Home schooled with little social contact, a calm and happy childhood spent discovering nature and a passion for tinkering.

This is the childhood of Louis Pouzin, born in 1931, the eldest son of an unlikely couple, who would go on to become a high-level engineer and to concoct, in the 1970s, a smart and simple system at the origin of the Internet.

The grandfather, Louis Champouret, was born in 1867 in Chantenay-Saint-Imbert (Nièvre). France was then ruled by Napoleon III, Russia by Tsar Alexander II and China by the Qing government. It was also the year of the Universal Exposition in Paris… and the Eiffel Tower did not yet exist.

1867 also saw the passing of a law making it mandatory for municipalities to maintain a public school and create a national diploma obliging all children to acquire a minimum level of skills: the *Certificat d'Études*.

Married to Marie Ville, born in 1876, Louis Champouret had three daughters, but no son to take over the sawmill. His eldest daughter, Jeanne, so bright, had still not found a husband by the time she was in her early thirties.

© Springer Nature Switzerland AG 2020
C. Lebrument, F. Soyez, *The Inventions of Louis Pouzin*,
https://doi.org/10.1007/978-3-030-34836-6_1

It must be said that she was confined to the house. Her devout Catholic parents considered all the village boys to be miscreants so no outings to the village, no friends. It was therefore the priest of Chantenay-Saint-Imbert who was mandated to solve the problem. He placed an advertisement in "Le Chasseur Français", a magazine that had done well in matchmaking. The call was heard by another priest, in the Drôme, who had just the person: young Fernand Pouzin, born in 1892 in Montmiral (Drôme).

Fernand was from the generation that served as cannon fodder for the 1914–18 World War. He fought and survived but suffered greatly, namely from diphtheria. Despite a strong constitution, he returned in poor condition. When he got back, his siblings were all more or less established, but he had no job and did not know what to do. He left for Argentina with a friend for business. Tired, just a few months after their arrival, his friend died in an accident. Alone, not speaking the language, Fernand returned home.

The French government launched a major census of the entire population in 1909 with genealogical details, occupation and place of residence. According to this register, the father, Eugène Pouzin, is noted as the "patron" of a "wooden house" just like the grandfather Champouret in Chantenay. That made Fernand a good candidate for the sawmill… and to marry Jeanne.

Nièvre-Drôme, they met each other, got along, and married.

Grandpa Champouret was quite a character. First, he didn't like his son-in-law and let him know it even though he is the one who had found him. Second, he was crazy about crafts and technology. He had one of the first cars in the canton, in the 1930s electrified the farm and sawmill with direct current and was the first to have a telephone line in the village, with the magic telephone number: 1 in Chantenay.

A geek before his time….

A year after the marriage, Louis Pouzin was born on April 20, 1931. A sister was born 18 months later. The couple worked hard to develop the sawmill and managed to overcome various economic crises in a sector where bankruptcies were frequent. Fernand became Patron (as stipulated in the 1909 census documents) following his father-in-law and managed the staff with tact and finesse, he was a humanist.

The extended family lived in the sawmill, a set of buildings located away from the village. To accommodate the numerous relatives, the historic farm building was raised independently of the sawmill building to form two distinct paces. The household was made up of parents, grandparents, a great-uncle, aunts, sister… and Louis, precocious, funny and clever and pampered by everyone, with his mother taking on his education very early. He did not go to school—all children of miscreants—but stayed at home, the chaplain of a nearby convent taking charge of his education when his mother was surpassed by her student.

Although of robust constitution, Louis was small and agile: a lonesome child who loved his life at the sawmill, surrounded by machines and tools and whose constant tinkering was fondly tolerated by all. He was close to nature, capable of spending weeks observing a colony of ants for pleasure. Two cows, a filly, a vegetable garden, piles of wood everywhere, for him it was paradise. This unique childhood gave him a lifelong taste for nature, hiking and a solid practical sense. Louis loves to tinker, repair, take apart, invent, his favorite Christmas gift is a box of Meccano. This was fortunate, given his homeschooling, lack of a social life or friends. He got along well with his sister but both children lived secluded lives. The Second World War made little change to the family's way of life, despite the occupying army requisitioning the sawmill and residing in the large building. Nonetheless life went on in the older, smaller house and the family lacked for nothing. As Louis tells it, bread and butter were available, albeit through bartering with the neighbors rather than from shops. With his father Louis learned solidarity. The adaptability and resourcefulness of Fernand during this period enabled him to provide food rations to distant cousins and friends who suffered from deprivation. He even went to Normandy, by train, to pick up a cousin escaped from the Service du Travail Obligatoire [Mandatory Labor Service] to take him back to the sawmill and hide him under the noses of the occupying forces, with the help of the Mayor of Chantenay-Saint-Imbert, who provided real fake ID cards.

1.2   High School Years in *Ginette*

Josephine, a religious aunt who later became the Mother Superior of the Sisters of Charity of Nevers, insisted that her nephew be educated in a "proper" establishment. The nearest one meeting the family's quality criteria was in Nevers, 33 km away, too far to live at home. It was Aunt Marie, who had remained single and devoted to the family, who took up residence there to take care of Louis, who was enrolled in the sixth grade at Saint-Cyr College, where he was provided with a classical education, including Latin and Greek.

From the very first day however she judged the level insufficient and had Louis moved directly to the next class. There he started by catching all the childhood illnesses he had been secluded from and spent his first 6 months in bed. He nonetheless finished at the top of his class, by a large margin. This was Louis' first taste of community life and friendship, and he developed an ability to maintain strong ties with others: his first classmate from Nevers, Michel P., is still among his closest friends. Middle school was when he discovered the Scouts and their values of solidarity and mutual assistance, camps and walks in nature, also allowing the young Pouzin to satisfy his passion for DIY.

At Saint-Cyr de Nevers Middle School, he sailed through his classes, always at the top, and shone with his memory, his logic and his gift for scientific subjects. His talent for math delighted his mother who very early on decided that he would enter the most prestigious of the great French engineering schools, Polytechnique, and give the come-uppance to a local authority. Polytechnique is the Holy Grail of the Grandes Écoles, with rules that were first laid down by Napoleon I. Students are soldiers who live in a boarding school in a historic building in the heart of Paris, it is a school reserved for the elite of French society. To integrate X, as it is called, students must be the best in all scientific disciplines but especially in mathematics and logic. Among the illustrious alumni are mathematicians (Benoît Mandelbrot, Henri Poincaré), presidents of the Republic (Sadi Carnot, Valéry Giscard d'Estaing), famous engineers such as the inventor of the Parisian metro, Fulgence Bienvenüe, and André Citroën, the renowned automobile manufacturer. But Louis' mother did not know that Polytechnique was also an excellent financial solution for the family, which still had a daughter to provide for. Fed housed and dressed, students were paid a good salary and became civil servants who were no longer a financial burden on their parents.

After the Baccalaureate, Louis was sent to a boarding school in Versailles, the Sainte Geneviève school, commonly known as "*Ginette*", a Jesuit school specialized in preparing for the Grandes Écoles. This entailed a significant financial cost for his family: travel, board and lodging, tuition. Nothing however was too dear for a child so precocious and a mother's dream of seeing him accepted at the most prestigious French school. Again, he was the youngest and smallest in his class and constantly had to battle for first place with another student during the 2 years of preparation for the entrance competitions. That is where Pouzin's ingenuity came into play: to do well at *Ginette* meant being able to take notes quickly. To retain his envied position of leader Louis learned stenography through correspondence courses, and very quickly was able to take notes in this shorthand, which was totally unreadable for the other students and gave him a clear edge over his classmates. This skill further served him as a young researcher at MIT in Cambridge where, to compensate for the slowness of the card punching staff, he learned the *Star System* method and acquired the appropriate typewriter. After 3 months he was able to type with his ten fingers, and, very quickly, to produce his own punched cards and articles.

At *Ginette*, selfless as he was, he willingly shared his knowledge with the less gifted students and quickly became the reference for what had been taught in class. Although he says he never felt any pressure on his status as top of the class, it was a good way to become popular.

He went home for the school holidays, at first. Despite the discipline of the Jesuits at school, Louis managed to experience Parisian life and dined often with the bourgeois families of his classmates. He discovered the jazz clubs, the film classics at the cinematheque, the museums… a life he could not have had in Nevers and even less in his village Chantenay.

1.3   The X Years

Accepted at Polytechnique, he had to be granted special dispensation as he was so young. The motto of the École Polytechnique, "militarized" by Napoleon I, is "*For the country, science and glory*".

In September 1950, he arrived in Paris as a boarder at the Polytechnique. Although geographically close to Versailles and *Ginette*, X was another world, located in the heart of the Quartier Latin, rue de la Montagne Sainte-Geneviève, in the center of the capital. At *Ginette* his classmates were all young people from good families, but they were mostly from Versailles. At Polytechnique it was different, the students—all boys—were integrated into a military school and received a "stipend" (a monthly income) making them financially independent from their families. They came from all over France, but almost all from the very prosperous families of the haute bourgeoisie.

Discovering Versailles at the beginning of the twentieth century was to discover the Versailles elite; to discover Paris was to discover the elite of all of France. His classmates introduced him to Paris, the city of light and to the gilded environment of the children of the upper classes with their "rallies" for meeting girls, and sometimes skipping classes for fun. X was a privileged place for an elite which even had its own vocabulary: the *Pitaines*, the *Gamma Point*, the *Khômiss*… a jargon to unite the community. Each cohort had its own color, Red or Yellow, a class number and lifelong relationships between students. A Polytechnician is on familiar terms with his peers regardless of age and rank, that's the rule.

To manage these generations of young, brilliant but undisciplined students, the management of Polytechnique delegated the organization of joyous doings—the *Bahutages*—to a group recognized by the administration, the *Khômiss*. Louis got involved and organized parties with his friends at the *Khômiss 50*… where he was in charge of the telephone. The X Telephone

Exchange system was managed by the Compagnie Industrielle du Téléphone (CIT) with Captain Bougé (X47) at its head, with whom Louis established friendly relations. It was this "*Pitaine*" who was later to suggest the choice of telco and CIT to the young graduate of X who followed his advice. Not in the Research and Development sector, but in the Manufacturing division, a potential DIY niche. The word computer did not exist yet and the only future in such a position seemed to be electronic calculation. This was considered a reckless choice and was strongly discouraged by the Polytechnique Career Office as a sector with no future.

The *Khômiss* was also an opportunity to develop each other's gifts to do the most stupid things while remaining within the social norms of society and the school. It was thanks to the talents of one of his fellow *Khômiss* students, Claude Sainte-Claire Deville, that the small group even managed to have TV nights: with parts swiped from the radar lab he built a television. In 1950, only 4000 French people had this privilege.

Louis was excellent at reproducing keys, locks had no secrets for him, so he was in charge of letting students in and out as they went out to sample the Paris night life. The places where one could sneak out were called the *Betas* (but Louis was the king of locks) and those who got caught went to the *micro-castle*, the school prison, to spend a few days, which led neither to duress nor infamy.

Among the school pranks is the story of the disappearing doors, spirited away while under the influence.

As Louis tells it: "*I was X50 and actively upheld the various traditions of the École Polytechnique, then located on the Montagne Sainte Geneviève in Paris.*

One of these traditions was the Khômiss whose role was to build an "X" identity: a group of a dozen students in charge of "perpetuating disorder and traditions". These "pitaines" are in charge of maintaining order among the students… but also of organizing pranks for pleasure or in retaliation against management abuses.

Among the duties of the Khômiss were the Beta: identifying illegal entry and exit points to and from school. Personally, I was very good at producing keys (real and fake).

During one of these adventures, we targeted the administration corridor. We had noticed that while the two doors at either end of this corridor remained permanently open, those of the administrators' offices were always closed. One night we removed all the doors from the offices and hid them in the cellars. Then we locked the doors at the ends of the corridor. The next day everyone was astounded, no one had ever seen those doors locked and no one knew where the keys were. Then, even more incredible, when they finally got the corridor doors unlocked, they found that all the office doors had vanished! After vigorous action on the part of management we finally confessed to where the doors were hidden, but they were big wooden doors, all different. It took several weeks for General Services to get each door back in its right place and for days we saw people lugging doors around, trying to find where they fit. Subsequently, management had each door engraved with a number, as a precaution…"

Five or six army corps were represented on campus to recruit future executives from this young elite. Activities were organized to introduce students to the specificities of each military career.

This is how the aeronautics officer—known as *Officer Avia*—took volunteers to the Istres base near Marseille whence the students discovered the fleet of aircrafts and set off on a discovery tour in Algeria and Morocco for a few weeks. During his first trip in 1950 Louis discovered Marrakech and Djama El Fna Place. Passionate about photography, he took pictures that are still in one of his trunks, scattered around his children's homes. The second year he returned to Marrakech, a city that had greatly impressed him and thought to bring his own photos… that he had taken care to develop in postcard format to send to his friends.

Marrakech housed a fighter pilot school. After this second trip, Louis returned home in the cockpit of the fighter aircraft, having been warned: "If you vomit, you clean the cockpit". Spins, spirals and other acrobatics figures abounded but, although green to the gills, the student managed to land without mishap.

The normal flights for these trips were noisy and lasted a long time, rarely managing more than 500 km a day. The craft was a JU52 (Junker 52), a single-engine aircraft with fixed landing gear, recovered from the Germans after the war.

The plane was the same age as Louis.

The students were strictly supervised during these outings, very unlike life in Paris at X. The officers kept the students to a tight schedule and taught them strict respect for military life. However, on the return from this second trip, a tire burst upon arrival in Istres and the students stayed a few days in the city, enjoying the evenings without supervision, creating very good memories.

But the École Polytechnique is a military school, with training and preparation for parades where the smallest are placed in the last row. This is for a square perspective to be respected and for the photos taken from the front to show a larger army. Since there were only seven or eight "small" ones, it was the competition to be the smallest and the least "selectable" to complete the ranks. Louis was excellent at escaping the drills and constraints of military parades.

Unfortunately, as Louis was prone to daydreaming, he forgot to wear the protective gear for his ears during training one day. The detonation of the weapons pierced his eardrum causing deafness that has only increased with age. He now has to wear a hearing aid.

This golden youth could have turned Louis Pouzin's head, being a young provincial still full of religion and raised in a strict environment where people had to work hard for a living. Fortunately, while he remained close to the religion of his childhood, he also encountered a hitherto unknown species: worker-priests. These were clergy, priests of the Catholic Church but integrated into professional life, often as salaried workers. Launched in the 1940s and 1950s, this movement was condemned by Pope Pius XII in 1954, but continued nonetheless.[1] These priests advocated values of mutual aid and solidarity that reminded Louis of his years as a Scout and the lessons of mutual support learned during the war.

From 1950, soon after he arrived at X, Louis, always curious about everything, became involved in humanitarian actions, a term unknown in France at the time and which would remain so until Abbé Pierre's appeal for the homeless in the winter of 1952. This is what allowed him to keep his feet on the ground and to have a clear view of the elite and the reality of post-war French society. Between talks and presentations of their activities, Louis was particularly interested in the actions of one of these priests who dedicated himself to helping the poor, Father Liégé. He was a Dominican priest who sought to introduce the young polytechnicians to other sections of the population, marginalized people, whom worker-priests at the time considered a little *sulphurous*, in need of care. Liégé knew them all and he was not ashamed to associate with them. He gave lectures on them at the school. There was a structure called "friendship teams" that were led by two Parisians with original personalities, and among these teams there was one which included a doctor who participated in the presentations. Louis began to frequent these groups, who met in the area near the École Polytechnique, in the rue Mouffetard and Place de la Contrescarpe. Compared to these dives into other facets of society, dance classes with girls from good families and flirting immediately seemed dull, especially since it was difficult to maintain social relations with a bourgeois elite while spending evenings and weekends on the streets with the poor... Louis was too aware of social disparities but also too inhibited by his religious education to have extensive relationships with girls.

---

[1] https://en.wikipedia.org/wiki/Worker-Priest

Much of the time I was at the Polytechnique, my only social life was through my colleagues from Saint Geneviève who invited us to "parties" with their families. There were girls to marry. In fact, my wife is the sister of one of my former classmates.

In this popular district in the center of Paris called "la Mouf'", which starts at Place de la Contrescarpe and goes down rue Mouffetard, Louis soon became one of the pillars of support for the poor young people and tramps. He formed strong friendships with the other volunteers and, while the other students went from social gatherings to private evenings, he organized marauds, outings and patrols, summer camps in the mountains and at the seaside. All these activities were undertaken during his school holidays, for the benefit young people who had mostly never left Paris or even their neighborhoods. A self-taught musician, Louis liked to play the pennywhistle (pipeau in French), an instrument that is easy to learn and inexpensive. He started during his camping trips when he was young and it became one of his trademarks, to such an extent that his close friends still call him "Pipo".

Going down rue Mouffetard with Louis and his then accomplice, Annie, is to go back in time. The rallying point at La Mouf was Monique Beauté and her bookstore, in front of which stood a Frenchfry stand. The friendships fostered in this period strongly marked Louis' personality: secret, iconoclast, sociable, supportive and faithful to his friends.

This is the case with his friend Robert with whom he shared many marauds and who found himself one day homeless in Paris. A poet and prolific writer,[2] Robert's muse was Paris.

At that time, Louis owned a small but very well-located apartment in Paris, on the Ile de la Cité. Robert occupied the apartment free of charge and stayed there for more than 10 years… "I didn't need it for myself, the family needed more than a square meter," explains Louis. To make his friend pay rent never even occurred to him, "he's a friend", he answers, surprised by the question. Robert and his wife, Irene are still among Louis' best friends.

Conquered by this vision of solidarity and always curious to discover the world, Louis even did a 3-week "worker internship" in a paint factory over the holidays where he filled paint pots, without revealing his status as an engineering student at the Polytechnique. He even went so far as to take a room in the 15th arrondissement so that his official address at the Polytechnique would not be revealed. But his mother wrote to him regularly and the landlady, intrigued by this young man who did not seem "normal" to her, opened them.

---

[2] Robert Belghanem self-published his 59th book in 2018.

She must have been surprised by how often the letters mentioned religion and insisted he continue to go to church. This stint as a worker was also an interesting human experience with the discovery of trade union activities including the distribution of leaflets… around the churches! But this did not prevent him from obeying his mother and continuing to attend Mass at Saint Séverin (at that time he lived at 2½, Quai des Grands Augustins, above the famous Lapérouse restaurant). He detached himself little by little from religion, but cautiously.

He continued his activist activities long after his school years, in fact for more than 10 years, when he was already in the world of work at the CIT, but never spoke of them because no one would have understood this social and solidarity commitment.

The frugal but flourishing life of his childhood has had a profound impact on his character—a penny saved is a penny earned: the principle of single-use disposable items displeases him greatly, things should be repaired, recycled. He is economical by nature and rules his daily life in accordance with these principles: eating little but well, drinking, yes, but only good wine. A healthy life, a time disrupted by his addiction to cigarettes, like many generations. The switch to cigars gave the inventor an additional trademark: a mischievous smile and a cigar dangling from his lip in most photos.

The notion of solidarity and sharing is still alive in Louis' mind, which also explains why he has always refused to patent or reserve for his own benefit the various technical inventions he has created throughout his life.

What about his studies? As a young adult discovering life, he realized that he didn't much like math, theorems were too rigid for this inventor. At the end of school, he was somewhat at a loose end and didn't know what path to choose. Students are ranked according to their results and it was popular to follow predetermined pathways: Finance, Administration, the Army… but none of that appealed to him.

He was among the top three when he entered the Polytechnique School but was ranked close the bottom at the end, and still with no chosen career.

1.4   Military Service

At the end of his education, before entering the world of work, he had to opt for an army specialty to complete his year of military service. He chose the Navy because it was clean: no mucking around in the mud. It wasn't much to ask for and he was lucky to be stationed in Toulon on the Montcalm cruiser. He spent a few months at the radar detection center in the Porquerolles

Islands, a magical place near Marseille that had not yet become fashionable. He was detailed to "plane vigil" (in fact, a deckchair) on the ship's deck, dined at the Pasha's table (the Commander) and was part of the crew sent to London on the Thames to take part in the festivities for the coronation of young Queen Elizabeth II, but without being allowed to land.

It was 1952, Louis was 21 years old, had graduated from the most famous French school, was "released from military service", he was now a young adult: his life lay before him.

2

Early Career (1952–1963)

2.1 From CIT to Bull

At the end of his military service in 1952, Louis Pouzin chose to return to civilian life,[1] and began a career in industry. That was the year that the young Pouzin joined the Compagnie Industrielle des Téléphones (CIT—Industrial Telephone Company) in Paris, which later became CIT-Alcatel, then Alcatel. This was a true industrial apprenticeship for the young engineer, who was in charge of machine manufacturing, receptioning parts and checking their quality. Louis says he was "*dragged there*" by his former telco manager from Polytechnique, who already worked there. "*I began in a methods office, with a large room and offices, department heads, foremen, small groups… It wasn't very exciting, but it was a good way to discover how the industry worked, in a company that manufactured telephone equipment, both switchboard and transmission equipment.*"[2] Around the age of twenty, he could easily have made his career in this telco subsidiary of the CGE (Compagnie Générale d'Electricité—General Electricity Company), climbed the rungs and participated in the development of the telephone industry in France…[3] but fate had other plans and quickly pushed him in a different direction, towards what the German

---

[1] Students who did not become civil servants at the end of their studies had to reimburse the State for their tuition fees. Louis paid for a few years until Bull paid off his debt.

[2] Interview with Louis Pouzin, December 27, 2016.

[3] Alain Kyberd, "L'État et les télécommunications en France et à l'étranger, 1837-1987", EPHE, Librairie Droz, 1991.

© Springer Nature Switzerland AG 2020
C. Lebrument, F. Soyez, *The Inventions of Louis Pouzin*,
https://doi.org/10.1007/978-3-030-34836-6_2

engineer Karl Steinbuch called, in 1957, "computer science", or "information processing".[4]

One morning in July 1956, like every morning, Louis was reading the daily newspaper *Le Monde*, when he chanced upon an intriguing article about first generation computers.[5] At the time machines were still equipped with rollers and cranks, thus programmable devices capable of performing thousands of operations per second[6] were fascinating to the 24-year-old engineer. The journalist of *Le Monde*, Jean Uvreur, wrote a rapturous article on the IBM 650, the first serially manufactured computer: "*launched on its amazing cogitations, it grinds columns of figures by the tens of thousands, like a grindstone with its millions of grains. (…) What is it not capable of? It has been made to play with these objects: determinant calculation, numerical integrations, Fourier analyses, function tables, coefficient tables, gradient calculations, analysis of variance, curve smoothing by the least squares method, crystal structure analyses, stress analyses, vibration analyses, optical paths, trajectory calculations, etc., and it has done it faster than polytechnicians.*" In 2012, during a discussion with the American historian Andrew Russel, Louis still remembered his emotions reading the article: "*something awoke in me. Something terrifically intellectually exciting.*"[7]

Three months later, at the Porte de Versailles in Paris, Louis rushed to the sixth edition of the SICOB (Salon des industries et du commerce de bureau—Trade Fair for Office Industries and Commerce)[8]—an event dedicated to IBM and Bull perforated card accounting machines and computers, the RAMAC 305 and the Gamma 3. Faced with these large aligned metal cabinets, not very aesthetic but highly impressive[9] it was love at first sight. So, when a few days later, again in *Le Monde*, he found a job posting from Bull, the French flagship of electronic computing which was looking for engineers, Louis Pouzin immediately sent in his resume as a polytechnician. *"At the time, I was very enthusiastic about mechanics. But when I discovered computer science, I immediately understood that the potential was much greater. Mechanics takes time, it requires the use of a lot of tools… whereas with computers, all you need is*

[4] Bernard Widrow, Reiner Hartenstein, Robert Hecht-Nielsen, "Eulogy", IEEE Computational Intelligence Society, August 2005, http://helios.informatik.uni-kl.de/euology.pdf

[5] Jean Uvreur, "En regardant travailler les 'monstres sacrés' de l'automation", Le Monde, July 18, 1956.

[6] The first computer systems used vacuum tubes for circuitry and magnetic drums for memory, and were often enormous, taking up entire rooms.

[7] "Oral history interview with Louis Pouzin by Andrew L. Russell", 2 avril 2012, Charles Babbage Institute, Center for the History of Information Technology University of Minnesota. http://hdl.handle.net/11299/155666

[8] Musée de l'informatique, projet "SICOB, les temps modernes", www.sicob.tv

[9] "RAMAC, l'ordinateur commercial capable de tenir une comptabilité complète", Le Monde, October 12, 1956.

a pencil to create a program and then do whatever you want!", he recalls with a smile.[10]

Out of his former classmates at "X", he was the only one interested in this new field of research, alongside the late Henry Leroy, designer in 1967 of a compiler for the Algol programming language, and the late Jean-Pierre Brulé, Bull's President in the 1970s. At first, things got bogged down, forcing the bubbling Louis to champ at the bit, and stay at the CIT: the Suez Canal crisis in the autumn of 1956 prevented French companies from hiring, starting with Bull: "*The company had decided to suspend induction because it feared a fuel shortage. They told me that I would be hired shortly after my interview, but as they feared that the industry would fail, hiring was suspended. So, I waited.*" His patience was finally rewarded. For 6 months, his resume remained on top of the recruiter's pile and at the beginning of 1957, when the crisis was over, he was immediately contacted for a new interview and hired.

2.2 From Bull to MIT

In February 1957, Louis Pouzin arrived at Bull's offices at 94 avenue Gambetta, in north-east Paris—not far from his small apartment, located rue de Vaucouleurs, in the heart of the former revolutionary Paris of the 11th arrondissement. At the time, when the young X engineer was taking his first steps in the company, the American IBM dominated the new IT sector with its first generation computer, the 650.[11] In the face of this hefty competition, Bull was developing an electronic computer, and gave Louis (just 26 years old) the task of managing a small technical division, and serving as a "bridge" between the company's sales engineers and technical management (which manufactured the equipment sold by the sales representatives), to design perforated tape readers. With 15 people under his command, including six "former" technicians "who already had a lot of experience" and thanks to whom he admits having "learned a lot", he provided support to the company's commercial division. "*The machine designed by Bull was supposed to be autonomous, but in reality, it had to be connected to a punch card machine, and it didn't have a permanent memory, he says. We were still a long way from the computer business!*" The war between Bull and IBM to dominate the new IT world quickly escalated and in 1960 the French company, which sold computers in 148

---

[10] Interview with Louis Pouzin, May 22, 2015.
[11] Charles J. Bashe, Lyle R. Johnson, John H. Palmer, Emerson W. Pugh, "IBM's Early Computers: A Technical History (History of Computing)", The MIT Press, 1986.

countries and had begun to catch up with its American competitor in France, wanted to *"make a big splash"*.

Facing the American giant and its first hard disk computer, the Ramac, it had already launched the Gamma 30, a computer of similar power.[12] But its objective was now to create "the ultimate French machine", intended in particular for scientific computing and insurance companies: The Gamma 60. This computer, one of the first in Europe to use transistor technology, the ancestor of the integrated circuit, needed to be programmed, a task that Bull quite naturally gave to Louis Pouzin, age 29 and already an old hat in IT. At the company's headquarters, rue Gambetta in Paris, he suddenly found himself at the head of a team of 30 engineers. "*The company had put a lot of resources into designing this huge machine, but it was the first-time engineers were programming, he recalls. Before, they managed teams and were not trained to program at all, because that was the technicians' job. Bull's technicians didn't have the right culture, it scared the hell out of them. So, they hired young graduates and gave them to me*". Having to manage a whole group of young people from elitist higher education institutes (Les Mines, X, Centrale, Arts et Métiers), but without experience and "dragging their feet, because it was an ungrateful task for them", Louis was a little frustrated. Especially because his job consisted more of management than actually developing. "*They were learning, but I didn't have time to guide them. I had to deal with administrative issues, get them salary increases and square meters to work in, plan the work… so I didn't have time for programming. I couldn't stay in this situation; it was unbearable for me!*"

Louis Pouzin, 31 years old, then turned his attention, with envy, to the many Americans who landed en masse at Bull, following the recent takeover by General Electric.[13] "*They came for a little tour of Europe to see what was going on at Bull, he says. And I could see that there was a lot to do in IT, it was a really promising field. My boss at Bull spoke English, like many sales engineers, so when they dealt with the Americans, they did so without me, because I didn't speak the language. If I didn't improve in this area, and if I didn't know more about programming, I risked being marginalized and frozen out of the future. So, I asked my boss if I could go to work in the United States for a while. He concurred, and agreed to find me a job there, allowing me to be seconded by Bull.*"

Before crossing the Atlantic Ocean, Louis Pouzin began to learn English. He took lessons at the Berlitz school, paid for by Bull, and in parallel applied an original learning technique, invented by Scottish teachers at Edinburgh

---

[12] Philippe Nieuwbourg, "Bull Gamma 30", Musée de l'Informatique, August 10, 2009, http://blog.museeinformatique.fr/Bull-Gamma-30_a217.html

[13] Georges Vieillard, "L'Affaire Bull", Chaix, 1969.

University: "*you had a tape recorder, you heard a sentence, you immediately repeated it and then listened to your own repetition. In parallel, the method consisted in reproducing sounds in English, using small diagrams representing the mouth, tongue and teeth. It was very convenient, and it worked…*".

3

The American Years (1963–1965)

3.1 Time Sharing

January 19, 1963. On a cold and snowy day, all alone, Louis Pouzin boarded a Boeing 707. Destination: The United States. He went to Cambridge, to work with the research team of the late lamented Fernando José Corbató,[1] deputy director of the computing center at MIT (Massachusetts Institute of Technology), the famous university and research institution specializing in science and technology. The two men had already met at the Fourth Congress of the International Federation for Information Processing (IFIP)[2] in Munich, on Tuesday, August 28, 1962. *"We were introduced by a mutual acquaintance from Bull, the director of the company's Electronic Computing Center, Philippe Dreyfus, who had been a professor of computer science at Harvard in the years 1943–1944. Professor Corbató told me about his work.[3] I didn't speak English very well, but we still exchanged for a moment, during which I told him, in my own way, that I was interested in his research and more than keen to go to the United States to work in his team. A few months later, he sent me a letter inviting me to join him as a system programmer."*

---

[1] "Fernando Corbató, a Father of Your Computer (and Your Password), Dies at 93", Katie Hafner, The New York Times, July 12, 2019, https://www.nytimes.com/2019/07/12/science/fernando-corbato-dead.html

[2] (International Federation for Information Processing - Fédération internationale du traitement de l'information).

[3] In 1990, Dr. Corbató received the A. M. Turing Award, widely considered the computing field's equivalent of the Nobel Prize.

© Springer Nature Switzerland AG 2020
C. Lebrument, F. Soyez, *The Inventions of Louis Pouzin*,
https://doi.org/10.1007/978-3-030-34836-6_3

Louis slept in a room at the Boston YMCA for a few weeks, before finding an apartment in Cambridge, near MIT, and then a pretty little three-floor house in the quiet Jamaica Plain district, one of the greenest areas in the city, with trees and lawns everywhere. He also bought a second-hand Peugeot 403. Meanwhile, in Paris, an American scientist replaced him, as part of an exchange program between researchers. On March 20, almost 3 months after his arrival, his young wife Isabelle and their two young children, Rémy (2 years old) and Anne (3 months old), joined him, still under the snow, after a short journey in a "car-trailer team" on icy roads. *"Isa was 19 years old when we were married in 1961. So, 11 years younger than me. She was the sister of one of my classmates, we met at a surprise party. At the time she was studying math and physics. But once we had children, she stopped her studies. She agreed to come to the United States. She was then 21 years old. For her, it was an interesting adventure"*, recalls Louis. The small French family, who spoke approximate English but were very friendly, quickly caused a sensation at MIT. *"We were a curiosity, everyone wanted to invite us over for dinner or drinks, so we quickly integrated that small world of geeks and researchers"*. But it was especially at work, when sitting in front of a machine, in the white light of the MIT computing center, that the French engineer amazed his colleagues.

Californian computer scientist of Portuguese origin Fernando Corbató, 37, was one of the most prominent specialists in Whirlwind,[4] the first "real-time" computer, designed in 1951 by MIT as part of a flight simulator project for the US Navy.[5] The man everyone called "Corby" and who won the Turing Prize in 1990[6] then worked in tandem with ARPA (Advanced Research Projects Agency),[7] on a "time sharing" project: the "MAC" (Multi Access Computer)[8] on an imposing mainframe computer, the IBM 7094, in a dedicated laboratory at the MIT Computation Center (the future Laboratory for Computer Science).Since 1961 the charismatic Corbató and his team of dedicated young computer scientists had been designing an operating system (OS)

---

[4] "Ainsi naquit l'informatique: histoire des hommes et des techniques", René Moreau, Bordas, 1987.

[5] Charles Babbage Institute, "Oral history interview with Fernando J. Corbató", 1990, http://hdl.handle.net/11299/107230

The Whirlwind was able to perform several functions in real time. It was at the origin of the machines used by the SAGE (Semi-Automatic Ground Environment) network, the United States Air Force's real-time radar system.

[6] Awarded by the Association for Computing Machinery (ACM), the Turing Award is presented annually to an individual selected for his or her (technical) contribution to the IT community.

[7] The Advanced Research Projects Agency is part of the US Department of Defense, independent of the armed services.

[8] Fernando J. Corbató, Marjorie Merwin-Daggett, Robert C. Daley, "An experimental time-sharing system", Spring Joint Computer / AFIPS Conference Proceedings, 1962. http://larch-www.lcs.mit.edu:8001/~corbato/sjcc62/

that could run on several machines at the same time: the CTSS (Compatible Time Sharing System).

"*The idea of time sharing*, explains Louis, *was to share a large machine between several programmers, in order to save time. By avoiding the machine being immobilized by a single developer, the process could be considerably accelerated.*" At the time the stakes were high, because time sharing was seen as the promise of interconnecting terminals, towards a networked IT system, no longer centralized. No more incompatible computers and computers not talking to each other, in theory. In any case, no more batch processing, which prevents a task from running before the previous one has finished—a process that can take between several hours and an entire day.[9] Henceforth, a computer would be accessible to several users, independent of their location.[10] In this context, Valérie Schafer, a historian specialized in digital technology and the origins of the Internet at the CNRS,[11] considers in her PhD thesis "La France en réseaux"[12] that "through its vision of interactive computing and resource sharing, the Project MAC foreshadowed some aspects of Arpanet", the data network that was to be developed between 1969 and 1971 by ARPA, and the ancestor of the Internet. In other words, for Louis Pouzin, to get involved in such a project meant going full steam ahead into the world of networks. For the young engineer, who has always loved to tinker and invent things since childhood in his father's sawmill, the Project MAC-CTSS was indeed an incredible opportunity. "*For me, it was an unexpected opportunity to program a powerful machine in a really concrete way! I was going to learn a new computer concept that seemed revolutionary to me, and which required me to write, to invent from scratch a program for machine management*".

3.2 The Project MAC

The project MAC belongs to a very particular political and geopolitical context. When Louis Pouzin arrived at the MIT Computing Center, John Fitzgerald Kennedy had been President of the United States for 2 years. The

---

[9] John A.N. Lee, Robert Rosin, "The Project MAC Interviews", IEEE Annals of the History of Computing, 1992.

[10] "Time-sharing: réalités et perspectives", Le Monde, October 11, 1966.

[11] The French National Center for Scientific Research (Centre national de la recherche scientifique, CNRS) is the largest governmental research organization in France and the largest fundamental science agency in Europe.

[12] Valérie Schafer—*La France en réseaux*, CIGREF, 2012. Digital Economy and Foresight Collection, ISSN 2111-6814.

young Democrat was then fighting the economic recession and had begun to improve the situation. The American economy had renewed with prosperity, and "JFK" was fighting poverty with his domestic policy, called "New Frontier". Internationally, Kennedy's foreign policy was dominated by tensions with the Soviet Union, manifested in Cold War struggles, particularly in the scientific field. In 1957, the Soviets put into orbit the Earth's first artificial satellite, Sputnik 1, and in 1961, Yuri Gagarin became the first man to enter outer space. In parallel, Kennedy was facing the failure of the Bay of Pigs invasion in Cuba (a botched attempt at a military invasion by US-backed Cuban exiles). To restore America's prestige, he launched an ambitious space policy aimed at getting American astronauts to walk on the Moon before the Russians. In parallel, the President of the United States was pursuing the policy of "a total and universal, political, intellectual and scientific struggle for freedom", initiated during the Korean War (1950–1953) by his predecessor, Dwight Eisenhower. On the technological front, a huge influx of investment by the Pentagon in research and development of new information technologies enabled the computer industry to take off between 1953 and 1961.

In 1959, nearly $1 billion in research and development contracts were awarded to American computer manufacturers. This figure is comparable to the total amount of computer purchases in civil markets in those years, and far exceeds any support given to the computer industry in other countries. It was at this time that IBM won a request for proposals that allowed it to outperform its competitors, designing the first transistor computer in 1959. IBM's 7000 series of mainframe computers are the first in the company to use transistors. The 7030 model, also known as the "Stretch", was then at the top of the range, and was built in 1961. It was also in 1961 that JFK logically gave his full support to time sharing systems experiments—starting with Fernando Corbató's project MAC. In other words, the project MAC was eminently strategic for the United States, at a time when researchers were multiplying inventions all over the world.

With five "system programmers", a profession still unknown in France, Louis Pouzin was initiated, with pleasure, into "machine code" (the native language of the computer's processor). The "startup" atmosphere—no hierarchy, great freedom of action—fit perfectly with the very flexible operating mode of the polytechnician engineer. "*Initiative was more than encouraged. In the team, we were all overexcited. Because we were creating something that had never been seen before: a time sharing operating system. And we held all the cards.*" The laboratory atmosphere was also very stimulating. The Project MAC's computer scientists worked near the university campus, then moved to the ninth floor of Tech Square. Located at 545 Main Street, Cambridge (a bustling student city which hosts both MIT and Harvard), this imposing building, "a paradise for hackers", houses both a computer research laboratory and an artificial intelligence laboratory (the future "AI Lab"). In the roar of machines and air conditioning, programmers rubbed shoulders with the pioneers of AI Marvin Minsky (inventor of the first randomly wired neural network learning machine) and John McCarthy (at the origin of LISP, the first computer programming language using symbols), as well as Richard Stallman, future initiator of the free software movement.[13]

Louis Pouzin worked closely with a young programmer from the MIT Computation Center, integrated into the MIT Project MAC immediately after her engineering studies: Glenda Schroeder. *"I remember the day Corby introduced us. I was delighted to share my office with such a charming man, and so… French! He had a really brilliant mind. I learned a lot from him because he was much more experienced than I was. He was a wonderful engineer and a great thinker"*, she recalls fondly.[14] Although, as Glenda says, the French computer scientist at the time spoke "rudimentary English", he quickly became part of the team: *"he made great progress in our language, and he quickly established himself as one of the leaders of the CTSS project. He was a true leader, with very innovative ideas."* Regarding the MAC Lab, the American engineer remembers a team of "hard workers", although very friendly, and an *"interesting combination of young people who had just graduated from university, students, computer professionals and MIT professors, such as Corby and Bob Graham, a computer scientist from the computer center of the University of Montréal"*. Meanwhile, Louis Pouzin *"was a professional… more credible than most of us, because we were just children"*, she says with a smile.

For a year, Louis and his teammates worked day and night, under the discreet supervision of Professor Corbató, a tall man who was always impeccable with his round ringed glasses and dandy suit: *"He was a very cultured person, with a rather particular sense of humor, very dry. We got along very well together,* recalls Louis. *He had a very rare quality: he managed to push us forward simply by listening to us talk, and by subtly guiding us, without us really realizing it. A true driving force for all of us. A very good boss"*. These are qualities that, a few years later, many young French researchers will also perceive in the French engineer, who also cultivates his appearance as an English dandy.

In early 1964, Louis and his colleagues at MIT finalized and officially created the CTSS, one of the very first timeshare operating systems. *"It worked both in batch processing and timesharing, he recalls. We could compile and debug,*

---

[13] Steven Levy, "Hackers: Heroes of the Computer Revolution", Globe, 1984/2013.
[14] Interview with Glenda Hughes, October 17, 2017.

while others were doing management or scientific calculations". One thing led to another and the polytechnician was entrusted with "increasingly strategic developments": in 1964, he participated in the design of the successor to CTSS, the Multics operating system.[15] *"This innovative operating system was designed to host several hundred users simultaneously,* he says. *It has become a symbol OS, often used to explain how a machine of the future could work, with a completely new memory management system"*.

3.3   The Birth of Shell Multics

During the design phase of Multics, the French engineer suggested to his colleagues that they design a command interpreter, to serve as a direct interface between the OS and the user: *"After writing dozens of commands for CTSS, I finally told myself that the commands should be usable as building blocks, which could be used to write new commands (like software libraries), and to automate this."*

At the beginning of 1965, he developed the RUNCOM program, an "interpreter" that makes it possible to execute a set of commands contained in a file, and makes parameter substitution possible.[16] *"This tool quickly became popular with the team, because all of a sudden they could go home in the evening while letting the control blocks run at night"*, recalls Louis. This new technique, which consists in using commands as a programming language, was dubbed "shell" by the French computer scientist.

"At that time, there was a significant division between OS and application programs. Louis changed that, allowing the OS to be accessed from a program, which then led him to the shell. His work was revolutionary, and it is the basis of the Multics system. It was a central part of the system, the key to the OS", says Glenda Schroeder thoughtfully. From the Project MAC, the computer scientist remembers that it "introduced the idea of a virtual memory, the idea of a

---

[15] Originally intended for General Electric GE 635 family General Electric computers, then used in the 1970s by the Honeywell 6180.

[16] "The Origin of the Shell", Louis Pouzin, Multicians web site, 2000. www.multicians.org/shell.html

command interpreter (with the shell), and the ability to work in multitask mode.[17] Things which are still found in computers today."[18]

In June 1965, the exchange program for researchers between MIT and Bull ended. Louis and his family packed their bags to return to France. Without being asked, the computer scientist left Glenda Schroeder and her "small group of witches" from the CTSS / Multics project, a technical note and a "flowchart" describing how to formalize his idea of the shell, in the future operating system. "*Thanks to Louis' instructions*, explains the software engineer,[19] *between 1966 and 1967, I was able to design a real programming language—the Multics shell[20] -, that would save time by centralizing and automating repetitive operations, such as reading commands, analyzing terms and calling subprograms. It was a real innovation, still used by many free systems, such as Unix, the descendant of Multics.*"

For Louis Pouzin, now 34 years old, the return to France was a personal relief, even though he was the one who had originally asked to leave in the spring of 1965. And despite Professor Corbato's regular requests for the French engineer to stay, he held his ground. "*I didn't want to live there, to settle there. I just wanted to get up to speed, professionally, in IT and English! I was really very happy professionally, the time sharing adventure was very exciting, but I didn't want my children to grow up in America, in a deeply hypocritical and politically correct society, where you have to stick to the script. I've never stuck to a script.[21] In addition to that, my wife, who was constantly at home and taking care*

---

[17] Computer multitasking is the concurrent execution of multiple tasks over a certain period of time. New tasks can interrupt ones already started before they finish, instead of waiting for them to end.

Indeed, before, CPU time was expensive, and peripherals were very slow. When a computer was running a program that needed access to a peripheral, the central processing unit (CPU) had to stop executing program instructions while the peripheral processed the data. It was generally very inefficient. The first computer using a multiprogramming system was the British "Leo III", owned by J. Lyons and Co, in 1961.

[18] "The scariest thing is that we have made the computer extremely easy to use. It will therefore be used more and more", Professor Corbato told John Fitch of the MIT Science Reporter in 1963 about Multics and Project MAC. "A Solution to Computer Bottlenecks"—Science Reporter TV Series: https://youtu.be/FTcLzZOQTvk

[19] Interview with Glenda Hughes, October 17, 2017.

[20] "Project MAC Progress Report", Volume 4, Massachusetts Institute of Technology, Advanced Research Projects Agency, July 1967, http://www.dtic.mil/dtic/tr/fulltext/u2/681342.pdf

[21] On this subject, John Day, an American researcher, former member of the Arpanet project, now a friend of Louis Pouzin's, with whom he is developing the RINA project (see later in the book), told us:

There were liberal enclaves in Boston at the time, but certainly not at MIT. Louis *was* correct, especially during this period. Boston didn't really begin to 'open up' until after the mid-1970s. It is still much less so than the Midwest. A friend left Silicon Valley and returned to New England for the same reason. Another friend found the same thing… about Europeans. Actually, Louis' description of American society at that time is not that different than an American's description of France.

of the children, suffered from loneliness and living away from her brothers and sisters. She was quite isolated in our home in Jamaica Plain. Unlike me, she was not entitled to the invasive drug of programming."

While he made friends in New England, Louis was disappointed to see that in the United States, friendly and social relationships are often short-lived. "*People there are very hospitable, but they change friends almost all the time, without making huge efforts to maintain their relationships. They spend six months together—a year, then move on to other people, and so on. A very sad vision of friendship…*" Although he has kept several friends in the United States, with whom he continues to correspond today, including Glenda Schroeder Hughes (who now lives in Palo Alto), Louis was not very sad to return to Paris. On the professional level, however, his outlook was different: he left the States starry-eyed. His work on timeshare was a revelation for him. "*Professionally, it was of course more interesting for me to stay in Boston than to return to Europe, but private life always comes before that kind of consideration! If I had stayed, I would have been sucked into the Multics project, which was supposed to be tested on a General Electric machine in the spring of 1965. I would have been stuck. So, I felt it was better if I left. But it was a great experience in any case*", he recalls with a touch of nostalgia in his voice. "*It was my first contact with real computing, with the idea of networks and data sharing. That's where my desire to network came from, no doubt.*"

4

Back to France (1966–1971)

4.1 An Ambassador of Time Sharing

After a short trip with Isabelle to Mexico in her Peugeot 403, then a visit (in France) to her "various family branches", Louis returned to Paris with his family. His apartment in the 11th arrondissement, rue de Vaucouleurs, was now too small for the family, and the Pouzins quickly moved into a larger apartment in Charenton-le-Pont, southeast of the capital. Back at Bull, the computer scientist was no longer really the same. For a few weeks he was up in the air as to his future professional activities, wanting to find a new project related to time sharing, but this time in Europe—hoping that Bull would "decide to enter the running". In the meantime, he reactivated his network, first his boss at Bull Paris, Jacques Pepin de Bonnerive, head of the company's "technical sales" team. Then, thanks to him, he quickly found something to bounce back on, by becoming the ambassador of timeshare. His experience at MI—almost 3 years of programming and time sharing, a real professional springboard— had transformed the young computer scientist, who now spoke English fluently, a great asset at Bull, a General Electric subsidiary since its acquisition in 1963. He was now a true expert in timeshare operating systems. *"In Boston, I was able to do things I could never have done in France, because the Americans give workers a lot of freedom of initiative. Over there, it's practice before concepts. So, I took some initiatives, for example by proposing to create a command prompt system for Multics (the shell). And I learned a lot."* In the eyes of his colleagues, he was a celebrity. *"I had become a star. I knew a lot about timesharing, I had finally surpassed my colleagues thanks to my experience in programming, and my new boss, Pier Abetti, took me on a tour of Europe to talk about time sharing and*

© Springer Nature Switzerland AG 2020
C. Lebrument, F. Soyez, *The Inventions of Louis Pouzin*,
https://doi.org/10.1007/978-3-030-34836-6_4

its benefits to the big companies to which Bull and General Electric wanted to sell machines, especially the GE 600 mainframe computer, which replaced the Gamma 60".[1]

Louis Pouzin became a great traveler: he journeyed back and forth between most European capitals (Rome, Stockholm, Berlin, London…) and the major cities of France. "*I had become the propagandist of time sharing. I made the presentations with large panels and markers*", he recalls with amusement. "*It allowed me to be recognized a little bit in France, especially in universities… because before, when we were engineers at Bull, engineers from an industrial company, we had no connection with academics. So, I found myself with very easy relationships with researchers: they were interested in going to the United States and working on time sharing because they didn't know what it was. Thus, at my level, I brought the communities closer together*". But in 1966, after a whole year of "touring Europe", and despite the pleasure of travelling, the Bull star trained at MIT began to get tired of it. "*I thought it was a little repetitive, I had experienced the position in full. It was always the same speech to companies—about the benefits of timeshare, which made it possible to develop programs much faster, in a few days instead of a few months*".[2]

4.2   The Météonome Project (Meteos)

Devoured by a desire for change, the 35-year-old hyperactive engineer, who was growing an impressive mustache, set out in search of a new, different project. Bull's management then proposed that he take charge of the unforeseen development of a time-sharing operating system and software for the GE 600, for use by the national weather service, the Direction de la Météorologie nationale (DMN), the ancestor of Météo-France. "*Originally, the latter had ordered a large machine from Bull to be able to make forecasts*", says Louis. "*The GE 600 was designed for conventional management, and it had to be adapted to the management of meteorological information, which circulated by telex from the north to the south of the country, and which had to be processed over time, depending on when it arrived.*"

For the computer scientist, this project was innovative: "*we felt that the world was going to change, it was something we had never seen before!*" He was quickly provided with a small laboratory at the National Meteorology Office, located just next to the Alma Bridge in Paris, and set up a small team of three

---

[1] "La gamme des ordinateurs Bull General Electric", Le Monde, October 11, 1966.
[2] "Time-sharing: réalités et perspectives", Le Monde, October 11, 1966.

engineers, assisted by five DMN researchers. "*When I started recruiting people for the weather, I placed an ad in the newspapers: 'Real Time Weather', and I was describing an operating system. I thought people would laugh, because there's nothing more improbable than real-time weather… But nobody reacted, I was a little disappointed*", he says, laughing. In order to be closer to his workplace, he moved at the same time with Isabelle and their children to the 15th arrondissement of Paris, rue de Presles, near the Parc of the Champ-de-Mars.

In 5 or 6 months, Louis and his team designed a timeshare OS that allowed the GE 600 (which he renamed "Météonome" after having slightly modified it) to release short, medium and long-term forecasts in due course. "*I used what I learned at MIT to design the system. The OS was very similar to CTSS and Multics*", he says.

But after 7 months of grueling work (day and night, as was his habit) that was beginning to bear fruit, General Electric, in the midst of financial collapse, decided that the GE 600 did not bring in enough money in Europe, and to stop marketing it. "*At the DMN, they were a little annoyed… They were forced to order another machine, but they also wanted to keep me, because they had already taken a liking to the operating system I was offering them. And I wanted to continue the project.*"

The computer ordered by the French Meteorological Service to replace the GE 600 was manufactured by Bull's American competitor, the Control Data Corporation.[3] "*This new machine was faster, but it had to be programmed, because there was only one of them at the time: at the SIA (Société d'Informatique Appliquée), a company founded by my former colleague Philippe Dreyfus… Besides, the weather guys wanted to keep me, obviously…. Then the general manager of Control Data in France, Gérard Beaugonin, a former engineer and colleague at Bull, went to see the manager of his former company and offered him arrangement deal: he would supply the computer, but Bull had to sing my praises and continue to work with our team on the Météonome. Of course, it was a resounding refusal. There was no way they were going to work with a competitor!*" Stuck, frustrated, Louis Pouzin gave himself a few weeks for reflection, and quickly reached a harsh conclusion. "*What really interested me was the work to be done, not the company. If the firm in which I worked slowed me down in my progress, I had no qualms about leaving*", he says. "*My goal was to create large systems*".

Crowned by his past experience at MIT, he was then contacted by many IT engineering service companies (SSII), who wanted him, and the DMN

---

[3] "Control Data en France 1963-1980s", Pierre-Éric Mounier-Kuhn, https://www.academia.edu/29429270/_Control_Data_en_France_1963-1980s_

contract. In the end he chose SACS (Société d'Analyse et de Conception de Systèmes—Systems analysis and design company), a service company dedicated to OS development for companies, which would later become Atos. This young IT service company was headed by Jean Carteron, an engineer and former head of EDF's (Electricity of France) computer center—which was once a Bull and its Gamma 60 customer. "*I knew him slightly, and he was also a polytechnician, X, like me. Someone very good, very competent, we understood each other very easily. We came to an agreement fairly quickly.*" In the spring of 1967, shortly before the birth of Gilles, his third child, Louis slammed the door on Bull, and the National Meteorology Department signed a contract with the SACS to work on a Control Data 6400. "*This machine was new (no one had been trained in its use in France) and quite original: instead of having a processor supplemented by peripheral parts, there was a single hardware processor, but which could be split into eight peripheral processors, which each contained the operating system. I analyzed all this, I saw how it worked, and I had the idea of creating an OS in the central processor, to enable time sharing*".

Without leaving the DMN headquarters, Louis Pouzin was now in charge of five IT specialists. Among them was Jean-Louis Grangé, a young system engineer who had just graduated from the Institut de Programmation (the computer science unit at the University of Paris VI), with whom he quickly became friends. Jean-Louis followed him later for further adventures—but we will come back to. "*It was an exciting project,* recalls the retired researcher. *The Meteonome was a new OS and computer, with 8 peripheral processors instead of just one… We were all delighted to be part of such an adventure. As for Louis, I immediately admired him. There was something awesome about him, he was a funny, intelligent person, with a rare sense of humor.*"[4]

This sense of humor also benefitted other students at the Institut de Programmation and Paris VI. Because at the same time, in parallel, the computer scientist began to give lectures, in an Amphitheatre—the very first ones given in France on the subject of operating systems. "*I was the first to do it. At that time, the other teachers spoke about programming in a more formal language, while I brought concrete information about systems. My students were taking notes… and it was these notes that then served as course material for other teachers at other universities for many years!*" Louis Pouzin's courses were initially quite informal: "*thanks to my research, I had come into contact with academics, they knew me, so they invited me to their meetings, to imagine the world of the future… We were discussing what to do in France in terms of IT, I was simply going there as a friend, because they knew that I knew the job well and that I was not a*

---

[4] Interview with Jean-Louis Grangé, February 13, 2017.

member of the establishment. And one day, these students invited me to give them lessons". Many of his courses on operating systems were based on the OS he was designing at the same time for the National Meteorological Office. For his students, everything the computer scientist taught was revolutionary. *"For them, it was completely new. Even though it was based on materials which already existed in the USA, their teachers had never made them read books on American machines or programming courses."* For the old "X", teaching was, at last, an opportunity to get back to serious work: *"teaching forces you to have a much more structured discourse on systems, and it also allows you to find new ideas".* It was this university environment full of new ideas, in May 68, that he would later draw on to find the many young recruits for his research teams. It was also during a student meeting that he met Maurice Allègre, a sign of fate. The future head of the Plan Calcul—a government plan to develop French and European IT, launched in 1966—and Louis Pouzin's hierarchical superior in the 1970s was then Robert Galley's deputy, the IT delegate to the Prime Minister, Georges Pompidou. *"He was a little heckled, and he had to leave the room that day",* Louis laughs. *"But meeting him served me well, sometime later…"*

During the Meteonome Project, the time sharing specialist learned a lot. *"In the end, I was able to work on machines with quite different structures, he explains. While often, even today, you still find talented computer scientists who have only one mental diagram of a machine in mind. They don't know how to change the machine structure, and they just replicate what they have already done".* At the beginning of 1969, after 2 years of work, the machine was completed. The DMN was satisfied—it used this time sharing system optimized for weather forecasting, "Meteos",[5] for at least 15 years. *"A record for an OS",* says the computer scientist. Finally, he continued, *"the weather no longer needed me, and the SACS, which still wanted to keep me, could no longer pay me, unless I accepted a position, essentially a commercial one, as a business engineer… which was really not possible for me. So, I had to find work elsewhere."*

4.3   The IT Department at SIMCA

In a newspaper, Louis came across a job posting from Simca—the "Société Industrielle de Mécanique et Carrosserie Automobile"—Industrial Company of Mechanics and Automotive Bodywork, an automobile manufacturer controlled by the American Chrysler—looking for an engineer capable of managing its IT department. *"The company was looking for someone to take care of*

---

[5] POUZIN, Louis - Le système METEOS. Revue l'Informatique, July 1970, n°6, p. 46–54.

'*real-time computer systems*': *this position was for me.*" At the company's head-quarters in Poissy (easily accessible by highway from the new house he had bought with his wife Isabelle, in Vaucresson, in the Hauts-de-Seine), the engineer was surrounded by Americans—but not really the same kind of Americans as those he had met in Boston and at Bull. "*The person who headed the IT department hired me mainly because I had worked at MIT. My mission at the computer center was to make the system work. But in this industrial environment, far from the universe to which I was accustomed, I quickly became disillusioned*". At Simca, he discovered life in a typical large capitalist company—with its specifications, its trade unions, its hierarchical system, its performance-oriented management methods, and its power struggles between departments—finance, purchasing, production, etc.—that he had never encountered before. "*On top of that, no one really cared about technical issues, they just wanted their computers—provided by IBM—to work in their factories, without worrying about the rest. It was anything but stimulating. No room for creativity.*"

Louis Pouzin really did not feel at home in the Simca environment (which became "Chrysler France" in 1970), where American managers were mainly looking to "cut off heads" and reduce budgets. He also passed, in the eyes of his colleagues, for a free spirit, far too rebellious to be honest. "*I threw out some unusual ideas that made the boss shudder.*" At the end of the 1960s was when "compatible" machines began to be manufactured—for example, IBM-compatible machines, but designed by other manufacturers. "*Some disk cabinets were faster and cheaper than IBM's. So, instead of only renting our equipment from this manufacturer, I ordered two cabinets from another American company. This obviously provoked the anger of IBM, which was then top dog at Simca. Fortunately, I was able to convince the company's director of the merits of my approach.*"

In the spring of 1970, when his second daughter, Stephanie, was born, he again came up against IBM when he attempted to allow the car manufacturer to follow in real time the production of cars in factories using a Time Sharing system, to use a ticker, a "teletype", not included in the catalogue of the American supplier.... All that needed to be done was to create an instruction to modify a 360 series computer to switch to master mode. "*The IBM guys took offense and tried to convince my boss that it was another very bad idea. But in the end, they just couldn't stomach the fact that their machine could be cracked so easily!*" Louis Pouzin also had confrontations with the "business experts" in Simca's "investment control department". "*Because additional telephone lines had to be installed to use these teletypes. After a study on costs, they told me 'it's your responsibility', I answered that this wouldn't be a problem... They were quite surprised by my answer! But connecting tickers to a computer was such a common-place thing for me that I couldn't see what the problem was."*

Tired of these perpetual fights, the polytechnician, who wanted above all to create and invent, started looking elsewhere once again. *"I was tired of all these quarrels between departments, between chiefs and deputy chiefs, who were only concerned with budgets. It wasn't the kind of career I was aiming for."* In leaving Simca, he left behind a new mindset. *"IBM was no longer the boss, they were put in their place!"* It was then 1971. *"I had worked at a lot of companies, so why not one more?"* Louis Pouzin didn't know it yet, but fate was about to push him much further than towards a new company—towards networks, in a project that marked the history of IT.

5

The Plan Calcul (1971–1979)

5.1 Louis Pouzin's Choice

In 1966, Charles de Gaulle, a former General who distinguished himself during the Second World War by leading the free France resistance from London, was President of the French Republic for 8 years; he was at the origin of the Fifth Republic which gives the President a role close to that of the kings of the Ancien Régime, and thus a firm hold on the reins of the country—to the point that his political opponents accused him of dictatorial ambitions. President Charles De Gaulle, who was re-elected in December 1965, had a unique vision of France's position in the world in the early 1960s. Everything he did, particularly in the field of international politics, aimed to serve the interests of France. For example, he used the European Economic Community (EEC, now the European Union) to help French farmers. Since the end of the Second World War, he had been wary of the United States and its influence, and also planned the gradual dissolution of the two US-USSR blocs. He pursued a policy of "national independence", which consisted of maximizing his distance from the major powers, the United States and the Soviet Union, while maintaining benevolent "cooperation" and "neutrality". He gradually reduced France's participation in NATO (North Atlantic Treaty Organization) until his withdrawal from military command in March 1966. While the USA was trying to restore its image, Charles de Gaulle's objective was to "restore France's status as a great power"—the similarities are surprisingly strong. It is therefore with this in mind that the French President reorganized the army, developing independent nuclear deterrence equipment, strengthening the country's economy, and launching several scientific projects. Among them, a

© Springer Nature Switzerland AG 2020
C. Lebrument, F. Soyez, *The Inventions of Louis Pouzin*,
https://doi.org/10.1007/978-3-030-34836-6_5

computer research program, the objective of which was to counterbalance the United States' "threatening" domination in computer science, to reduce France's dependence on the US, and create a "European industry" for the manufacture of computers and software. At that time, De Gaulle (then his Prime Minister and successor, Georges Pompidou, who continued his policy from 1969 to 1974) and his advisers became aware of the future importance of information technology in many fields (medicine, media, science, etc.), like chemistry or energy; while in the United States, scientists were preparing to send men to the Moon, creating intercontinental ballistic missiles and miniaturizing electronics with transistors.

In 1966, Bull dominated the French IT sector, but was still up against the giant IBM. Faced with "Big Blue", the French company, which was experiencing financial setbacks, merged with the American company General Electric. Pierre-Éric Mounier-Kuhn, IT historian, tells us: "*Until 1963, Bull, a small family company that became a multinational corporation, had had a faultless track record… But it made a serious mistake by marketing a computer it did not control the development of: the Gamma 60*".[1] This machine, on which Louis Pouzin had worked as a programmer, was a commercial failure, leading the company into serious financial difficulties. "*In the spring of 1964, Bull decided to sell a controlling interest to GE, in exchange for providing them with cash and turning them into its sales network in continental Europe. One could say that the company was then saved but it was a great shock for the French government, which was also reeling from the White House's refusal to deliver the only machines which would enable it to set up a real nuclear program. At that time, we finally considered the computer as a machine for communicating and processing information, and no longer as a simple calculator*", notes Valérie Schafer.[2] The transfer of Bull (Europe's leading manufacturer of information processing machines) under GE's control was perceived as a slap in the face by electronics engineers, technocrats and Gaullists. "*The reaction was to sidestep Bull, to continue to look for a French solution to the IT problem in the country, even if it meant merging small companies, none of which had any serious experience in business IT or international commercial sales*", notes Pierre-Éric Mounier-Kuhn.

At that time, IT became a strategic, even vital, domain for France. "*Europe was losing ground to the United States in this area. However, in the early 1960s, computers were no longer just used for research calculations, but were used operationally by the military as part of large computerized air defense networks.*" In France, Georges Pompidou and Charles de Gaulle launched the "Plan Calcul",

---

[1] Interview with Pierre-Éric Mounier-Kuhn, April 18, 2017.
[2] Interview with Valérie Schafer, December 1, 2016.

designed to "ensure the country's autonomy" in information technologies. *"The public authorities had perceived that IT was an up-and-coming sector, and considered that France, without a strong or structured industry, could not be absent from this movement and had to make up for lost time. The government therefore decided to mobilize large sums of money and to entrust them to a small team: the Délégation Générale à l'Informatique (general delegation for computer science)"*, recalls Philippe Renard, a former member of this organization, created in September 1966 to build a French computer industry. The objectives of the DGI were to stimulate the production and use of software and computers for administrations and companies, and to lobby investors.[3] In parallel, in December 1966, as part of the Plan Calcul, a private company was set up for the manufacture of computers and software—following the merger of CAE (Compagnie Européenne d'Automatisme Electronique), a subsidiary of CGE, CSF (Compagnie Générale de Teleégraphie Sans Fil), and SEA (Société d'Electronique et d'Automatisme), a subsidiary of Schneider. This new company was named the "Compagnie internationale pour l'informatique" (International Computer Company), CII. Supported by the DGI (which managed the budgets and projects within the Plan Calcul) and financed by State subsidies, its mission was to develop IT for both scientific research and management, to stand up to the computer manufacturers Control Data, IBM and Bull-GE. *"It was a real technocratic solution, difficult to manage, because we were merging two SMEs that hated each other (SEA and CAE), and asking them to create 4 or 5 computers in 2 years, the equivalent of what IBM had barely managed to do over the previous 4 years with the IBM 360 range"*, says Pierre-Éric Mounier-Kuhn. The challenge was huge. With the CII and the DGI, the French were promoting their industrial IT strategy, but the Plan Calcul still lacked a research component. The government therefore created the IRIA (Institut National de Recherche en Informatique et en Automatique—National Research Institute for Computer Science and Automation).[4] This research and teaching center was also a way to better train civil servants in the field of information technology.

"In a context where IBM held 80% of the market and was a master of the IT industry, we (a small team in the DGI) wanted (with significant resources provided by the State, but with relatively weak expertise and training) to build a company that would make products as good as IBM's", says Philippe Renard. As a young engineer on loan by EDF to the DGI, he was then in charge of

---

[3] Pierre-Éric Mounier-Kuhn, "Le Plan Calcul, Bull et l'industrie des composants: les contradictions d'une stratégie", Revue historique, 1995.
[4] Tristan Gaston-Breton, "Le plan Calcul, l'échec d'une ambition", Les Echos, July 20, 2012.

"software" projects. Within the DGI, he was in charge of financing software development at the CII, which led him to travel to the United States several times to meet manufacturers and service companies. In 1969, with the late Michel Monpetit, one of the heads of the Delegation and future deputy director of IRIA (while in Paris, former Prime Minister Georges Pompidou became president, after Charles De Gaulle resigned[5]), he left to "*see what new things were happening*" across the Atlantic. He traveled to Lexington, Massachusetts, among other places. At MIT's Lincoln Laboratory, a laboratory of the Department of Defense Research Agency,[6] he met the engineer Larry Roberts, who was head of the Arpanet,[7] a computer network project which was still in the experimental phase but had already linked up the machines of 4 university centers working with ARPA: the University of California at Los Angeles (UCLA) and at Santa Barbara (UCSB), the Stanford Research Institute in Palo Alto, and the University of Utah, in Salt Lake City.

The architecture of this data transmission network had been in development since 1968 under the leadership of the US Department of Defense and President Lyndon Johnson, who succeeded John Fitzgerald Kennedy, who was murdered in November 1963 in Dallas. The Advanced Research Project Agency Network was supposed to link most computer centers in the United States, but also in Europe, starting in London, where the British Donald Watts Davies, of the National Physical Laboratory (NPL), had been developing a distributed computer network concept using the time-sharing method, since 1965. It should be noted that since 1962, in addition to financing Fernando Corbato's project MAC, ARPA had been working on a project to connect the computers of its research centers, as well as those of contracted universities—not only to secure military communication networks in the event of war, but also to facilitate the sharing of resources and data. In parallel with Donald Davies, MIT researcher Lawrence Roberts had been working

---

[5] In 1968, France experienced a major social uprising among workers and students. When the situation was finally settled in 1969, De Gaulle consulted the French people in a referendum on Senate reform, but it was rejected by 52% of the votes. In fact, voters were not so much in opposition to this reform than they were weary after 11 years of "Gaullian" presidency. On April 27, 1969, General de Gaulle assumed his failure and resigned. On June 15, Georges Pompidou, Prime Minister under De Gaulle between 1962 and 1968, was elected President of the French Republic. He continued the general's policy, which he shared, but broke with France's diplomatic isolation after his election: he was sincerely pro-European and supported the development of the EEC, and although he continued the "Gaullian" policy of independence, he made it more flexible, more friendly towards the United States, as well as towards the United Kingdom, which he accepted for entry into the EEC in 1973. At the national level, like De Gaulle, he wanted to modernize France, in particular through the Plan Calcul. At the same time, he had to face the 1973 oil crisis and its economic repercussions.

[6] Advanced Research Project Agency (ARPA).

[7] Advanced Research Projects Agency Network.

since 1966 for the US Army and its "Information Processing Techniques Office" (IPTO) on an offshore computer network project, the objective of which was officially to serve all projects sponsored by the US government, but is also, informally, to move digital data through several different channels, so that the whole would not suffer too much in the event of the destruction of one or more computer centers—especially in the context of a potential conflict with the USSR. This network project led by the ARPA has its roots in the rivalry between the USA and the Soviet Union which had been launched in the 1950s, from the space race to scientific competition. Arpanet, which benefited in 1969 from colossal investments by the American government, is one of the many projects designed to strengthen the prestige of the United States in the world.

"*When I came back to France, I told my colleagues at the DGI that it was absolutely essential to do something similar and to finance development activities in the field of networks. The idea spread rapidly, from the DGI to the IRIA, until the formalization in 1970 of a network project, a kind of French Arpanet*". The DGI's goal was not however to compete with Arpanet. Politically, the aim was for the CII to distinguish itself from the heavyweights Siemens and Philips, with which it had recently formed an international consortium to create a powerful range of European IT products: Unidata.[8] "*While Philips was an electronics expert and Siemens dominated the mechanical peripherals sector, the CII still had to find its specialty, its masterpiece in a way…*", says Louis Pouzin. For the CII to succeed, it needed a niche project, where it could become the leading expert in certain skills. With the DGI and IRIA, the company then chose the strategic area of networks.[9]

"*The idea was to carry out a very sophisticated project, which would satisfy the growing need for digital networks in France and Europe. At the time, there were already quite a few networks, military and for data (SNCF [the national railway company], insurance groups, banks, etc.), and these large organizations wanted to interconnect their computers within networks*", explains Pierre-Éric Mounier-Kuhn. "*On the other hand, many companies and administrations had developed databases: The Ministry of Public Works, the Ministry of Research, the Ministry of National Education… However, a database is only of interest if a maximum number of users have access to it, hence the obvious usefulness of networking them*". According to a survey by the Interministerial Commission on Informatics, there were about 20 databases in France at that time, and information

---

[8] Pascal Griset, "Informatique, politique industrielle, Europe: entre plan calcul et unidata", Institut d'histoire de l'industrie, Rive Droite, 1998.

[9] Jacques Jublin et Jean-Michel Quatrepoint, "French ordinateurs", Editions Alain Moreau, 1976.

exchange was often difficult, if not impossible, at least in digital form. Being able to interconnect these databases would make it possible to promote exchanges between administrations, but also to make savings, by using a network adapted to data transport, independent of that of the "PTT"[10] dedicated to telephone calls. In the United States, the Arpanet project relied on the real-time transfer of data sets, packets, rather than on traditional electronic circuit communication. For Louis Pouzin, an expert in timeshare, passionate about networks and the ARPA project, the progress of which he followed closely in scientific journals, creating a European version of this network would be entirely feasible. But at that time, in 1970, he still didn't know what fate had in store for him. In fact, he was just starting to consider leaving Simca which he found too rigid and stifling…

November 1971. To set up its experimental computer network, the DGI needed a project manager. But it was difficult to find the rare gem at IRIA: the research at the center based in Rocquencourt, in the Yvelines, did not concern networks at all, but technical and management computing, as well as applied mathematics and automation.[11] A few years earlier, in 1966, in Paris, Philippe Renard had attended a conference held by Louis Pouzin, when he was still advertising Time Sharing for Bull-GE. *"He was very funny: he used punch cards on which he wrote the main elements of his presentations. But apart from this eccentric side, he was a showman, an expert who mastered his subject, charismatic and totally fascinating"*. In front of a crowd of curious people, the French computer scientist gave a surprising speech for someone who had just spent 3 years in the United States, with resolutely militant accents: *"we must resist IBM's domination, and we must not use its technical solutions just because it represents 80% of the market."* This powerful speech stuck in the mind of the former head of the DGI. *"And when much later, at IRIA, we discussed who in France could be a potential leader of this network project, I put forward the name of Louis Pouzin"*.

After his experience at MIT and National Meteorology, the engineer, a little hesitant after his departure from Simca, enjoyed a flattering reputation as a *"competent guy, who makes systems"*.[12] His connections in scientific circles, in the United States and in Northern Europe, his skills and his wish to leave

---

[10] The "Postes, Télégraphes et Téléphones "or "PTT", was the French public administration responsible for mail and telegraphs and then telephones, in the nineteenth and twentieth centuries. As the State reformed, it was transformed into two public service companies: France Télécom in 1988 and La Poste in 1991, as well as regulatory bodies—General Regulations Directorate (DRG), which became the telecommunications regulatory authority (ART) and the Electronic Communications and Posts Regulatory Authority (ARCEP).

[11] Valérie Schafer, Op. Cit.

[12] Valérie Schafer, Op. Cit.

Simca made him the perfect candidate for the DGI and IRIA's network project. At the end of November 1971, he received a call from François Sallé, a former colleague at Bull who had been poached by the CII,[13] and then another call from Louis Bolliet, director of the CII research center and researcher at the IMAG (Institut de mathématiques appliquées de Grenoble—Institute of applied mathematics). *"They both told me, in confidential tones, that the DGI would soon set up a network similar to the Arpanet"*. A few weeks later, in December, Maurice Allègre, the director of the DGI, officially asked him by phone, then in person, to join the IRIA project. *"I didn't hesitate for a second: I said yes, yes, three times yes!"*

5.2 From Arpanet to Cyclades

In December, Louis Pouzin, who still lived in Vaucresson, enthusiastically arrived (via the highway) at Rocquencourt, at the Voluceau camp, in the former headquarters of the American army in Europe (SHAPE, Supreme Headquarters Allied Powers Europe)—a huge complex of military barracks all along the Marly forest, and which, 5 years earlier, had housed NATO's Command Structure. An employment contract was signed with the DGI (the engineer would only be paid by IRIA in 1973), which financed the project.

But before he could start, Louis, who was given the title of "technical director", first had to gather together a team, from scratch. And there was no question of drawing on IRIA researchers, whose profiles were far too removed from networks. Experienced in HR, Louis immediately mobilized his network and recruited half a dozen people on his own—a small team, as in the Meteonome era. First of all, he seduced a weapons engineer, a polytechnician like himself: the late Hubert Zimmermann. The man, who quickly became his right-hand man and a close friend, worked at SEFT (Section d'études et de fabrication des télécommunications de l'Armée de terre—Section for researching and manufacturing Army Telecommunications), where he had just completed the Sycomore project, the purpose of which was to create command systems for the Ministry of Defense. *"He was looking for an interesting project, and was thinking of going to the United States to develop his knowledge of networks… I met him through fellow researchers, and I managed to convince him that he could do it in France, by my side. I explained to him that what he was*

---

[13] A former head of a team of software developers, François Sallé was the central director in charge of Honeywell Bull's product policy at the end of 1970, shortly after the merger between Bull-GE and Honeywell.

going in search of in the United States, we were going to do here", remembers Louis Pouzin. Several years later, sporting mustaches and beards, like network musketeers, they worked together within IFIP and INWG (International Network Working Group) to standardize Internet protocols at international level. At CII, they also developed a layered network architecture, the Distributed System Architecture (DSI), which led to the design of the first version of the OSI computer communications model.

"*I also, as usual, called on old acquaintances.*" The second engineer recruited by Louis Pouzin was his former colleague from the SACS and the National Meteorology center, the young Jean-Louis Grangé. "*He asked me to join him at Simca in 1970, then this time at IRIA… I really appreciated that he asked me to follow him like that, twice in a row*", explains the latter, who ended up having a "quasi-subsidiary" relationship with his mentor. The trio thus formed was added to through the publication of an advertisement in the newspapers. Among the 60 resumes that he received within a few weeks, Louis chose only one: the late Jean Le Bihan, 32 years old at the time. He had graduated from Supelec (École supérieure d'électricité—higher institute of electricity) in 1968 and was an army scientist during his national service. He designed the very first real-time systems for French airports. Finally, the computer scientist borrowed three other talented young engineers from the CII, Philippe Chailley, Michel Elie, as well as a former teacher turned computer scientist, Jean-Pierre Touchard.

At the beginning of 1972, the small brigade thus formed was divided into two sub-teams—a group dedicated to the network itself (called Mitranet), led by Jean-Louis Grangé, and another specialized in the development of communication protocols, software and common interfaces, entrusted to Hubert Zimmermann. Then the team moved to IRIA. As Valérie Schafer writes in "La France en réseaux", the project led by Louis Pouzin was, at the time, "marginal" within the young institute that hosted it. In this "catalyst for French research", which until now had not carried out any network research, the seven computer scientists stood out and "felt a little isolated"[14] within SESORI—the "Service de synthèse et d'orientation de la recherche en informatique"—synthesis and orientation service for computer research, headed by the former Deputy Director of DGI, Michel Monpetit, in charge of liaising with the Plan Calcul, having for mission to launch projects leading to products that could be used by industry.[15] Louis and his team's work was quite

---

[14] Valérie Schafer, Op. Cit.

[15] Alain Beltran and Pascal Griset, "Histoire d'un pionnier de l'informatique: 40 ans de recherche à l'INRIA", EDP Sciences, 2007.

different from that of the research projects traditionally carried out at IRIA: several teams, some of which were destined to be set up elsewhere in France (particularly in the few universities at the forefront of computer science— Toulouse, Grenoble and Rennes), were expected to build, within 3 years, with the support of the CII, a network of computers that could be tested and then quickly transformed into an industrial prototype. That's why Louis Pouzin and his team had an entire building especially dedicated to their "pilot project"—freed after the relocation of an earlier project dating back to IRIA's previous boss, Michel Laudet, recently replaced by André Danzin. "*The latter was also a polytechnician. A former Executive Vice President and General Manager of Thomson CSF and in charge of the CII, he had both industrial experience and a strong presence, in addition to be a hard worker. He was perfect to both run a research center, and to talk to people about politics... He built relationships between IRIA and research centers (here and abroad), which helped us a lot afterwards*", says Louis. His former teammate Jean-Louis Grangé remembers with a big smile the IRIA headquarters in Rocquencourt (three rows of long rectangular buildings), and the stimulating atmosphere that prevailed there.[16] "*Given that the American military, then NATO members, once lived there with their families, it was a bit like a huge campus, with everything you needed: tennis courts, a sauna, a gym, a chapel, a canteen, and even a swimming pool. And there were dozens of computer scientists and pioneering engineers in their respective fields, each one more brilliant than the next... It was almost the same atmosphere as in Silicon Valley at the same time*".[17]

Louis Pouzin and his engineers quickly took ownership of the DGI and IRIA network project. The computer scientist gave it a name: *Cyclades*— named after a famous Greek archipelago, made up of 250 islands forming a circle in the Aegean Sea. "*Just as it takes boats to connect these islands, so it takes a system to connect the scattered centers of the future network*", he laughs. As Maurice Allègre, Director of the DGI in 1974, stated with emphasis, "*the main thing to remember is the image: processing centers remain isolated islands in the middle of an ocean of data overwhelming our civilization. Now, thanks to the network, these islands can be linked to each other and thus participate in a vast circle of information exchanges that will determine the future development of our society*".[18]

---

[16] Ibid, p.

[17] Interview with Jean-Louis Grangé, 13 February 2017.

[18] Presentation by Maurice Allègre, DGI, presentation of Cyclades to the government, February 8, 1974, INRIA, 02.00.013.

5.2.1   1972/An Agreement with the PTT/Packet Switching

Its team constituted; the Cyclades project could officially be launched. But first, the DGI had to reach an agreement with the Centre National d'Etudes des Télécommunications (CNET), the "Telecom laboratory", in order to use PTT lines and modems free of charge. In June 1972, the head of the "Direction Générale des Télécommunications" (DGT—Directorate-General for Telecommunications) Louis-Joseph Libois and the Director of DGI, Maurice Allègre, went further by deciding to have the CNET and IRIA teams work together. It must be said that over the previous year, the PTT research laboratory had also been building a data network, called *Hermès*. As the objectives of CCETT (Centre Commun d'Etudes de Télévision et de Télécommunications—Common center for television and telecommunications studies, based in Rennes), DGT and DGI were similar, it made more sense to collaborate than to compete. According to the agreement, Cyclades' telecom and IT professionals would work together to build a single switching system for their respective networks.   But very quickly, the cordial understanding shattered. While telecom engineers and IRIA IT specialists initially met and collaborated, they quickly came up against technical issues—in particular how to move data from one machine to another. PTT, like the Cyclades team, were strong advocates of packet switching,[19] a revolutionary method of transmitting information garnered from several trips to the United States and England by members of the DGI and CNET computer scientists, wishing to find a more economical and efficient way than installing a point-to-point line between each computer. Packet switching was theorized and invented at about the same time, in the early 1960s, by several different teams of researchers in the United States and the United Kingdom: the Americans Leonard Kleinrock[20] and Paul Baran, respectively based at UCLA and the RAND Corporation (Army Research and Development Center), which implemented it through the Arpanet nodes in 1969 and the British Donald Davies, of the National Physical Laboratory (NPL) in Teddington, who presented his concept in August 1968 at the IFIP Edinburgh Conference,[21] and who translated it into a network in 1970, dubbed the "NPL Network", or "Mark I".[22] As Valérie Schafer explains, "*contrary to circuit switching, which consists in*

---

[19] In a packet-switched network, data is transmitted in small pieces and routed independently between intermediate "nodes".

[20] "Information flow in large communication nets", Leonard Kleinrock, MIT, May 31, 1961.

[21] Luke Collins, "Network pioneer remembered", Engineering & Technology, IET, September 6, 2008.

[22] "The early history of packet switching in the UK", Peter Kirstein (University College London), History of Communications, IEEE Communications Magazine, March 2009.

allocating circuits for data transfer throughout the duration of the communication of the circuits, and which constitutes for each requester a reserved lane for the duration of the transaction, in packet switching, messages are cut up and pass from switch to switch. Such a system allows optimal use of transmission lines by sharing between users. A line is allocated to a user only for the time necessary to transmit a packet to the next node." A method that allows, in the case of time sharing and several messages circulating at the same time, *"a message contained in a single packet to arrive faster and to not have to queue behind longer messages with several packets".*[23]

While they were all convinced of the value of packet switching, PTT and IRIA engineers were unable to agree on the concrete way in which data should be transported. Packet switching is possible in two different forms: "virtual circuits" (VC) and "independent packets". With the first mode, all packets of the same message are sent in a single large stream. They follow a path (a virtual circuit), between the origin node and the destination node, and arrive in the order in which they were transmitted, according to the principle of sequential routing. With the second mode, independent packets, dubbed "datagrams" by the Norwegian telco engineer Halvor Bothner-By in 1975, are sent alone, "without connection", and not within a message flow. Each isolated packet is thus processed independently of the others and does not necessarily arrive in the same order as they were sent: all datagrams are then put back in sequence, and the message cut up at the start is reassembled upon arrival.

In the United States, Arpanet and the networks based on its protocol (NCP, Network Control Program), such as SATNET, Packet Radio Net and PRNET, used a hybrid mode, combining virtual circuits and datagrams. It was thus a case of packet switching with adaptive routing: messages are sent one behind the other, in a packet flow; then when they arrive at the first node, they are segmented and sent separately. Elsewhere, at the NPL and CNET, the Mark I and Hermès networks were based entirely on virtual circuits. This was obviously not the choice of the "Cyclamen", as the Cyclades engineers called themselves. *"Packet switching appeared to be a good solution for the digital networks of the future… but the Hermès network developed at CNET used the concept of virtual circuits, replacing physical telecom circuits, while Louis Pouzin and his team quickly came up with the idea of setting up a datagram system, which fulfilled the same function but in a more flexible way. We were always trying to have the most economical network possible, the fastest and safest operation possible",*

---

[23] "The Cyclades network and the Internet: what opportunities for France in the 1970s", Valérie Schafer, CHEFF, High Technology seminar, March 14, 2007, https://www.economie.gouv.fr/files/schafer-reseau-cyclades.pdf

summarizes Pierre-Éric Mounier-Kuhn. "*So, the PTT and the Cyclades team developed different standards. It was one or the other, no compromise was possible, there was no half-measure between these two technical formulas*".

Before going any further in the history of Cyclades, a focus on the power of the PTTs in the 1960s and 1970s is required. The Telecommunications Corps (one of the French technical "grand corps de l'Etat", main state bodies in France), created at the beginning of the twentieth century to develop a telephone network in France, became very powerful between 1920 and 1950. As Michel Atten, a telecommunications researcher explained at a conference in 2010, the French elites were appalled to discover the power of American telephone equipment during the First World War: "*the war led to the discovery of the technical and technological wonders of the "research branch" of Western Electric, the subsidiary that manufactures American Telephone & Telegraph (AT&T) equipment—equipment temporarily installed in France to serve the Allies by the American army. This makes the French aware of the delay in the French telephone network*".[24] The administration of PTT (as this ministry in charge of the post, but also of telecommunications in France, was nicknamed) was modernized, and the "State Engineers of the Telecommunications" multiplied. During the Second World War, Vichy and then the Fourth Republic created a telecommunications research centre, the CNET, and a general directorate for telecommunications, the DGT. In the 1960s and 1970s, the PTT occupied a very singular monopoly position in the field of telephone equipment. For example, in the United States, the Federal Communications Commission (FCC), an agency "independent" of the US government, is responsible for regulating telecommunications and communication services over telephone lines. It controls the rates that companies charge, and the equipment and services they offer. At the same time, one of these companies, AT&T, a direct descendent of Graham Bell's Bell Telephone Company (inventor of the telephone in 1874), is in a monopoly position, as it controls almost all telephone services (telephones, equipment) in the United States, renting them at a golden price to its customers. But AT&T remains a private, commercial company, which has no connection with the FCC. In France, on the other hand, the situation is quite different. The PTT are both a state structure like the FCC—this division of the "Ministry of Posts and Telecommunications" controls all telephone lines in the country—and a public service that rents its services to companies… as powerful and in a monopoly situation as AT&T in

---

[24] "The Telecommunications engineers in France: Networks, innovation and territories (nineteenth to twentieth centuries)". Symposium of October 21 and 22, 2010—Institute of Public Management and Economic Development, Feb. 4, 2014; https://books.google.com/books/about/Les_ing%C3%A9nieurs_des_T%C3%A9l%C3%A9communications.html

the USA. Today, PTT no longer exist. The DGT, which became France Telecom in 1988 and then Orange in 2013, was privatized in 1998 by Lionel Jospin's socialist government, then the French government sold a large part of its shares in 2004. It is no longer a state industrial service in a monopoly situation, but a private telecommunications operator, a commercial company, a consumer service provider—which is still very powerful in terms of telephone and Internet access, but which also faces other powerful French companies, such as Free, SFR and Bouygues—competitors who, as a very unique feature, use Orange's "Copper Network". This network, which covers the entire French territory, can be connected to the telephone and the Internet, and can be subleased by competing telecommunications companies. In the 1960s and 1970s, however, any project (public or private) related to telecommunications in France had to apply to the PTT, obtain their authorization, and pay a sum of money to them to use their equipment—without any possible recourse to a competing company. While also knowing that the quality of the PTT lines was often deplorable, as reported by some Cyclades engineers. A mediocre quality that was at the time the target of ridicule from several French comedians, such as Fernand Raynaud, according to whom *"in the 1960s, half of the French were waiting for a dial tone while the other half was waiting for the telephone"*.[25] It is for this reason that in the 1970s, the PTT and the French government multiplied innovative research projects aimed at changing this disastrous image—including the project Cyclades and its competitor, Hermès.

5.2.2   1972–1973/Datagram/Sliding Windows/ International Collaborations

After settling in Rocquencourt at the beginning of 1972, Louis Pouzin, 41, recruited his men, then immediately set off for the United States. Thrilled by his new project, his first reflex was to go around the world again to gather information, be inspired by the state of the art, and find ideas at the heart of research centers using Arpanet. He met Larry Roberts and Barry Wessler, two researchers strongly involved in the design of the American network, as well as Leonard Kleinrock, co-inventor of packet switching, also very involved in the ARPA project—it was the UCLA computer on which he was working that constituted the first interconnected node in Arpanet in September 1969.

After seeing his friend Fernando Corbató at MIT again, Louis returned to France at the end of February with the idea of designing a system for Cyclades

---

[25] Sketch "22 à Asnières", Fernand Raynaud, 1966. For example, most French citizens had to wait about 18 months to open a private telephone line.

based on packet switching, but with a network *"that would be interconnectable with all the other networks of its kind, whatever the technology, with the same exchange interface being the sole condition: the idea was therefore to consider it as a set of networks and not as a single network"*. This system of switching packets and interconnected networks via gateways, this heterogeneous network that would connect machines whose operating systems, programming languages and manufacturers would not necessarily be the same, was called the Catenet, which means "chain" in Greek.[26] In Louis Pouzin's mind, the Catenet would also one day make it possible to interconnect the other networks currently being designed in the United States (Arpanet) and Europe (NPL Net). It was this concept of "network of networks", which had not yet been created in 1972, that inspired Vint Cerf a few years later as part of an ambitious project: moving from Arpanet to the Internet (which literally means "inter network", or "network of networks").[27]

March 1972. Now it remained for Louis Pouzin and his group to find a communication protocol. After observing the Arpanet system in the United States, based on a mixture of virtual circuits and individual packets, as well as the NPL network in the United Kingdom, the computer scientist remained doubtful: *"why transmit packets in sequence, even if it is not until the very end, when it is quite possible to send them out of order and put them in order later?"* As the engineer explains, *"everyone I met in the USA found our project interesting… except BBN, who at first thought we were going to buy their network, Arpanet! (laughs) Instead, I rented one of their engineers, who came for a week every 3 or 4 months… We had a lot of practical information on how to implement things, but we also found that we could do things differently from them, that we didn't have to copy them, and that we could make our network simpler and more efficient."* In consultation with his colleagues from Cyclades, Hubert Zimmermann and Jean-Louis Grangé, he had the idea of using only independent packets, and entrusting flow control and transmission error correction to an end-to-end protocol—a method of circulating packets in the network that was completely at odds with the telecommunications system. *"While at CNET, the operators had reproduced the phone in the software—before starting to communicate, it was necessary to establish a communication mobilizing physical resources in each of the nodes crossed by the network -, we had a much more computer-based approach, a much more computer-based philosophy, with dynamic resource sharing, and the idea that it didn't matter if we lost packets in the network,*

---

[26] Louis Pouzin, "A Proposal for Interconnecting Packet Switching Networks", Proceedings of EUROCOMP, Bronel University, May 1974, pp. 1023–36.

[27] IEN 48, The Catenet Model for Internetworking, Vint Cerf, DARPA/IPTO, July 1978, www.rfc-editor.org/ien/ien48.txt

as long as a protocol recovered them", says Jean-Louis Grangé. According to the computer scientist, "*this idea was in the air, in the spirit of the times, but it had not been exploited until then, since even Arpanet was using a hybrid system… While datagrams made it possible to create an extremely simple and more efficient network, since we no longer had to worry about congestion problems.*"

Louis Pouzin and his team were imagining a two-level architecture for the Cyclades network, Mitranet, explains Jean-Louis Grangé: "*a packet exchange protocol with the best possible routing inside, and a transport protocol from computers to computers, which put things in order, and interfaced with the programs running inside those computers. This protocol was called SP1, then SP2, using the concept of datagrams.*"

At a "High Technology" seminar organized by the CHEFF (Committee for the Economic and Financial History of France) in 2007, Valérie Schafer asked herself in front of her audience: "*four nodes had already been built in Arpanet in 1969, and about fifteen centers were already connected to this network in 1971, when Cyclades started. Was there anything exclusively French in Cyclades, as compared to Arpanet? Was it just a copy of the American project or did they go further?*" For the historian, there was indeed French creativity, an innovation on the part of Louis Pouzin and his team. "*The Cyclades team first considered the datagrams. In the Arpanet project, the initial choice was hybrid and the first NCP protocol was based on a combination of these two concepts, before the TCP/IP (Transport Control Protocol—Internet Protocol) adopted the 'pure' datagrams, the path Cyclades had chosen*".[28]

According to her, French computer scientists also played a "significant role" in computer architectures, with the "seven-layer" OSI model (Open Systems Interconnection), which defines protocols that allow computers to communicate within a heterogeneous network. A seven-layer communication model, on which Hubert Zimmermann worked intensively between 1971 and 1978, within ISO (International Organization for Standardization), where he was in charge of the "Computer Architecture" working group. "*In this model, protocols are defined at specific levels: the transport layer, the link layer, the application layer, etc. The Cyclades team contributed to the definition of this seven-layer OSI model. They are not the ones who invented the layers, they were conceived at the University of Eindhoven by the Dutchman Edsger Wybe Dijkstra. The idea was also taken up in the Arpanet project, but with a four-layer model, layers 3 and 4 of the OSI model ("network" and "transport") that the French were supporting*

---

[28] "Le réseau Cyclades et Internet: quelles opportunités pour la france des années 1970?", Valérie Schafer, CHEFF, séminaire Haute Technologie, March 14, 2007, https://www.economie.gouv.fr/files/schafer-reseau-cyclades.pdf

corresponding to the TCP/IP protocol of the Internet network", notes the network history specialist. In 1972, no network had yet been designed based exclusively on independent packets: the Cyclades project was the first to attempt to fully apply this concept. "*Conceptually, the datagrams, which were called packets at the time, were there from the beginning, except that they were not used. No one had created a network based on this before us. What existed were virtual circuits… and the idea of packets, expressed on paper by Paul Baran, of the RAND Corporation (Army Research and Development Center), for Arpanet, but never realized before Cyclades—because the American network mixed virtual circuits and datagrams*", says Louis Pouzin. That is why, 1 year later, in the winter of 1973, after having carried out its first public demonstrations of Cyclades (4 computers were then connected by a first node) at the second European seminar on IRIA networks in Venice, the third Data Communications Symposium in Tampa, Florida, and finally in front of the Ministers for Industry and PTT in Paris,[29] the computer scientist claimed the status of inventor of the datagram, or "data packet transmitted in connectionless mode".[30]

When describing this system of isolated packets, the engineer systematically uses the analogy of postcards: "*rather than sending data in sequence on a pre-established channel, like train cars, the idea was to send packets like postcards. The packets have a destination address, and they move through the network accordingly.*" A datagram is thus a "*packet including its own destination address*". Each time it passes through a network node (a router), "*it is directed in the most optimal direction by the network itself, with the nodes constantly communicating and exchanging information on packet addresses*". This system works thanks to a transport protocol that "*uses the information contained in the packet*". The destination address can "*be located inside or outside the network, for example if it is a client's computer*". According to the computer scientist, independent packets were a good way to easily build a reliable and cost-effective network: "*This means that packet switches have much less work to do. There are several possible paths, which allows you to pass through several networks in parallel…*" It is this system, independent of the quality of service of the networks, that is now used on the Internet.

Were PTT afraid of competition and the IRIA project? In the summer of 1972, at least, a discreet wrestling match seemed to be taking place. While the

---

[29] Alain Beltran and Pascal Griset, "Histoire d'un pionnier de l'informatique: 40 ans de recherche à l'INRIA", EDP Sciences, 2007.

[30] As a reporter for the New York Times and Wired wrote in 2013: "Donald Davies had done simulations that used something similar to datagrams, but with Cyclades, Louis Pouzin was the first to make it a reality."

https://www.wired.com/2013/01/louis-pouzin-internet-hall/

Cyclades team was beginning to develop the Catenet, CNET engineers were forcibly programming a PDP-11 computer (from Digital Equipment Corporation, not CII) to make it the very first node of the future experimental network of the Hermès project, intended to work with virtual circuits: the "RCP", for "réseau à commutation par paquets—packet-switched network".[31]

"When I started Cyclades, I went out to meet all the people who had to be involved in it—the men from the CEA,[32] academics, industrialists, etc. They almost all agreed to work with us. But the PTT were closed from the beginning… What they had not told Maurice Allègre was that they had started developing a small network on their own—which obviously did not please the director of the DGI. Especially because the equipment used by the carriers did not come from the CII, but from the Digital Equipment Corporation (DEC), an American company. My project on the contrary was to build our network with CII equipment, so we were politically clear… except with regard to the PTT, because they didn't want to stop their own project. They wanted to make a network based on virtual circuits, which were already outdated technology for me at the time", recalls Louis Pouzin.In the autumn of 1972, the Cyclades project team grew and expanded outside the Paris region. For the past 3 years, Gérard Le Lann, a computer scientist who had graduated from the University of Rennes and the ENSEEIHT[33] in Toulouse, had worked at CERN[34] in Geneva, as part of a team designing a local network, composed of eight minicomputers, around the particle accelerator of the European laboratory—in order to allow the physicists' experiments to be monitored. Benefiting, as a result of this project, from a good "network culture", the engineer wished to broaden his horizons and get involved in research on the subject, so talked about it to everyone around him. He contacted Claude Kaiser, a polytechnician, with whom he had worked on a time sharing project during his military service. Like Jean Le Bihan, Gérard Le Lann was a contingent scientist and participated in the design of a real-time system at the Navy's programming center, the Coelacanth, in 1966. This project, led by the armament engineer Claude Kaiser, brought

---

[31] The experimental RCP network opened in 1974 after 2 years of studies and served until 1978 as a demonstrator for the future Transpac commercial network: http://a3c7.fr/w/index.php?title=R%C3%A9seau_exp%C3%A9rimental_RCP

[32] The French Alternative Energies and Atomic Energy Commission (CEA) is a key player in research, development and innovation in four main areas: defense and security, low carbon energies (nuclear and renewable energies), technological research for industry, fundamental research in the physical sciences and life sciences. http://www.cea.fr/english

[33] École nationale supérieure d'électrotechnique, d'électronique, d'informatique, d'hydraulique et des télécommunications—National Higher Institution of Electrical Engineering, Electronics, Computer Science, Hydraulics and Telecommunications.

[34] Conseil européen pour la recherche nucléaire—European Council for Nuclear Research.

together about forty scientists from the contingent, engineers and technicians from STCAN (Section Technique des Constructions et Armes Navales— Technical Section for Construction and Naval Weapons) and Maritime Engineering, in order to program an OS for the first French nuclear submarine, "*Le Redoutable*". It was therefore quite naturally that Claude Kaiser, who became a member of an IRIA project in 1972 to design an experimental time-sharing system, ESOPE, spoke to Gérard Le Lann from Cyclades. The encounter took place in August. "*Louis told me: 'I'm interested in your profile, you already have a network culture, you speak English, it's a perfect fit. I need a team in Rennes and I would like to put you in charge of creating a Cyclades team there, and because Arpanet is one of the sources of our inspiration, you will have the opportunity to go to the United States to visit the major network centers there and, if you can get an offer, I would not mind it if you spent a gap year at one of them*", recounts the Breton engineer.[35] In September 1972, he left for the University of Rennes to form a small delocalized Cyclades team—designed to simulate the network and computer communication protocols developed at Rocquencourt.

Between 1973 and 1975, Louis Pouzin also recruited many young engineers working in service companies such as SACS, Cap Sogeti and SESA: "*these companies were all interested in this network project, and in exchange for my promise to take them as subcontractors (developers), I could borrow high-level, full-time employees to be trained on my team*". Years later, most of these recruits participated in the French network projects. "*At the time, when there was a network to be built, for example for Air France or customs, the contract was awarded to a French company, but this was purely a facade, in reality the work was subcontracted to an American company. After our adventure, all network projects were carried out by French companies and not American ones.*"

5.3   Cigale's Connections

In October 1972, an engineer from the CNRS finally came to IRIA: Bernard Nivelet, who became head of the institute's computing center—including the machines connected to the Cyclades packet switching network, Mitranet, recently renamed Cigale.[36] "*At the time, using 66 kilobit links provided by the PTT, it interconnected the IRIA CII Mitra 15 computers with those of the*

---

[35] Interview with Gérard Le Lann, December 9, 2016.

[36] According to Louis Pouzin, "some politicians" found Mitranet's suffix "net" too Anglo-Saxon, and "not French enough". See "How the Web was Born", Robert Cailliau and James Gillies, Oxford University Press, 2000, p. 38.

universities of Rennes, Toulouse and Grenoble (CII and IBM machines). And because our project was to dialogue with the NPL and create a European network, we also set up a line connecting us to Rome and London", says the man who became Bull France's technical director in 1984. The Cyclades team even went so far as to imagine linking Cigale to an inter-campus network developed by the University of Waterloo, in Ontario, the CANUnet (Canadian University Network)—before it was stopped in its tracks by the Canadian Ministry of Communications (MDC).[37]

At the University of Rennes, within the Mitranet network's modeling and performance measurement center, which studied data flow regulation, Gérard Le Lann corresponded for several months with Leonard Kleinrock at UCLA, who had become a prominent figure in the Arpanet community, in order to enrich his research into "bizarre and inexplicable dysfunctions" (communication blockages, connection losses, desynchronizations) affecting the first Cyclades protocols. During the winter of 1972, in collaboration with Louis Pouzin and the teams of Jean-Louis Grangé and Hubert Zimmermann, he designed a simulator in Simula-67 (Simple Universal Language) to examine the problem more closely: *"it allowed me to create models of network nodes and connected stations, and to observe their behavior over time, when they were executed under the Arpanet NCP protocol and under the Cyclades protocol"*. Thanks to his simulations, the young computer scientist found a solution to the "problems of desynchronization between communicating entities", by imagining a mechanism of "sliding windows"—a system that, in the spring of 1973, allowed the Cyclades team in Rocquencourt to create a second, more reliable version of its protocol, which was integrated several years later (using the "pure datagram" mode) into the design of TCP, Arpanet's new transport protocol.

In April 1973, Louis Pouzin, who had just turned 42, sent Gérard Le Lann to the United States. *"I reminded him of his initial idea of making me work there for a year. He was very generous and suggested that I visit the Arpanet centers before choosing where to stay"*. After meeting Bob Kahn, the American project manager in Washington, then Leonard Kleinrock and Vinton Cerf, the Breton engineer chose to join the latter in Stanford. From June 1973 to May 1974, the engineer of the Cyclades project thus helped Arpanet researchers to improve their own communication protocol, while feeding his colleagues in Rocquencourt with ideas from across the Atlantic.

---

[37] "A network from coast to coast—The network that did not emerge", CA∗net Institute, 2001, http://www.cvm.qc.ca/mlaflam/Comm_e/Intro/historiqueInternetCanada.pdf

5.4   The IRIA Years

Cyclades was definitely an open project, fueled by international collaboration. From the end of 1972, American engineers began to work with the "Cyclamen" at IRIA to compare systems, measure performance, experiment with new formulas and draw inspiration from French research. "*They began to receive a lot of people from the Arpanet team and other universities… whereas until then, researchers' movements only went in one direction, with French engineers going to the United States to learn computer science and automation*", says Pierre-Éric Mounier-Kuhn.[38] In his view these exchanges between the Cyclades and Arpanet teams "*prove that the French had caught up technically, in less than 2 years*".

"*Until then, trips were made by French people to the United States, and a consulting contract had even been signed with BBN (Bolt, Beranek and Newman), the company behind Arpanet's subnetwork, to allow IRIA researchers to see what was happening across the Atlantic and receive advice. In 1973, there was a shift, and this time it was BBN engineers who came to IRIA to observe the functioning of Mitranet / Cigale*", says Valérie Schafer.[39] In Stanford, Gérard Le Lann also acted as an intermediary between Cyclades and Arpanet. "*For the year he was there he served as matchmaker, enabling close cooperation between the teams of Cerf-Kahn and Pouzin. And constant exchanges at international computer conferences also took place. At Arpanet's first public demonstration on October 24, 1972 in Washington, Louis Pouzin and his colleagues were on site*", the Internet historian adds. The two network projects never competed, but enriched each other: "*there was no competition, but on the contrary, there was even a node project between Arpanet and Cyclades*".[40]

The industrial stakes were high on both sides, "*but in this 'Republic of computer scientists', the teams worked together and talked to each other. They had a common objective: to create protocols and, ultimately, a network of networks*". Finally, for Arpanet researchers, the small team of French engineers proved providential: "*they were very happy to see Louis Pouzin and his men set up a network derived from Arpanet in Europe. Because in developing the Arpanet, they had been forced to focus on a number of technical solutions, and they would have liked to explore other techniques, other architectural formulas. With the Cyclades*

---

[38] Interview with Pierre-Éric Mounier-Kuhn, April 18, 2017.

[39] Interview with Valérie Schafer, December 1, 2016.

[40] A Cyclades—Arpanet link was thus envisaged in 1972, but according to Valérie Schafer, "the cost of such a link (13 million francs over 3 years) was considered excessive by Michel Monpetit. Nor was it politically obvious, in the context of the Plan Calcul, to support the idea of a link between the United States and France."

team, it was possible to experiment alternative ways, make comparisons, see the respective performances produced by the different formulas… Basically, we could do international research in a cutting-edge field. It was a win-win situation", explains Pierre-Éric Mounier-Kuhn.

5.4.1   1973–1974/Cyclades at the Top/A United Team/ Louis Pouzin, the Impeller

The first official demonstration of Cyclades and its packet-switched network, Cigale, took place in November 1973 in Paris, before the top brass—among them, Jean Charbonnel, Minister of Industrial and Scientific Development, and Hubert Germain, Minister of Posts and Telecommunications. *"We demonstrated to them that we could enter an order at Rocquencourt and send it to Grenoble to execute it; whereas in Rocquencourt, it was a CII machine, and in Grenoble, we used an IBM machine"*, recalls Louis Pouzin.[41] As described by historians Alain Beltran and Pascal Griset in "Histoire d'un pionnier de l'informatique: 40 ans de recherche à l'INRIA—History of a computer pioneer: 40 years of research at INRIA",[42] four computers, connected by the first node, were then interconnected (in Rocquencourt, Rennes, Grenoble and Toulouse), but very quickly, at the beginning of 1974, *"about fifteen centers were connected to the network"*—among them, the Institute of Computer Science and Applied Mathematics in Grenoble (Imag), the Saint-Étienne Mining School, the Rennes Higher Electrical School, and the Transport Research Institute (IRT), in Joinville (Haute-Marne).

At the end of 1973, tensions were still mounting with CNET engineers, who continued to develop their own network, Hermès—the future Transpac -, which was based on virtual circuits and not on datagrams.[43] Under these conditions, there was no longer any question of working together on a shared system. Looking for someone to make a decision, Cyclades IT specialists and PTT telecom engineers looked for an international guarantee. This is why Louis Pouzin came into contact with most of the teams designing or having designed networks—the Arpanet network, of course, but also the Tymnet of the time-sharing company Tymshare in California, CANUnet in Canada and

---

[41] Alain Beltran and Pascal Griset, "Histoire d'un pionnier de l'informatique: 40 ans de recherche à l'INRIA", EDP Sciences, 2007.

[42] BELTRAN, A./GRISET, P. – *Histoire d'un pionnier de l'informatique: 40 ans de recherche à l'INRIA*, EDP Sciences, 2007.

[43] "Du projet Hermès à Transpac", Alain Profit and Philippe Picard, Entreprises et Histoire, ISSN 1161–2770, N° 29, 2002.

the NPL Net in the United Kingdom. Cooperation was even set up with the Milan Polytechnic Institute and the Dutch Ministry of Hydrology who were interested in creating networks and connecting them to Cigale. That is why, in 1974, the Cyclades team also held a series of symposia, conferences and international events, where dozens of researchers and network specialists regularly met—from the National Computer Conference (NCC) in Chicago in May, to the sixth IFIP congress in August in Stockholm, to the second European seminar on networks organized by IRIA in Darmstadt in October. "*These congresses were an opportunity for both presentations and demonstrations*", writes Valérie Schafer in "La France en réseaux".[44]

With a touch of nostalgia, Jean-Louis Grangé describes a Cyclades project that took on a flagship role on the international scene in computer networking. "*We worked a lot with the Americans, we ended up signing a collaboration contract with them on the packet switching part, and I went very often to the United States, to BBN. At that time, we worked like crazy, but above all, we travelled a lot, all over the world*". Conferences and publications abounded. "*We, the Pouzin boys, presented the Cyclades project, the Cigale network, the protocols… All this in the wake of Louis, who was a true star at the time. He had an absolutely remarkable talent for public presentations, which were always a hit wherever he went. Because he was very funny, intelligent, and often very provocative*". The engineer says that among European and American researchers, "*the Cyclades team and project were very well known, and the conferences on the subject were eagerly looked forward to*". In April 1974, a month before the Chicago NCC, Louis Pouzin wrote to Maurice Allègre at DGI to say that Cyclades was "*now known to network specialists*". He also informed him that at international conferences, French computer scientists were perceived as "*leaders, an experimental source alongside Arpanet*".

With a little smile, Louis Pouzin remembers that the Cyclades project team at the time remained "on the fringes" within the IRIA itself, but this time for reasons of notoriety: "*we published a lot, we were known in our field, we were taken seriously at the international level. Logically, there was jealousy on the part of the 'true scientists', the mathematicians of the LABORIA (Laboratoire de recherche d'informatique et d'automatique—Computer science and automation research laboratory, specialized in applied mathematics, systems modeling and numerical analysis), directed by Jacques-Louis Lions, a mathematician… We tried to work together, but the relationship with Lions was ambiguous, because for him, anyone who is not a mathematician is not really serious. But our international success was a source of great interest for his own team.*"

---

[44] "La France en réseaux", Valérie Schafer, Nuvis, 2012.

International conferences implied incessant travel for Louis Pouzin… who also worked day and night on the Cyclades project. Stephanie, his daughter, runs a vineyard and has always kept away from computers. She was only 4 or 5 years old at that time, but she still remembers that her father was almost permanently jet-lagged because of his very frequent travels to America. *"Sometimes, I would get up around 1:00 in the morning, and he was always at his desk. And in the morning, when we went to school, he was just getting up"*, she laughs. *"My father was someone who loved to work and worked all the time. He would come home, eat, and then get back to work. Apart from the daily reading of Le Monde, he never did anything but work. But he was never stressed out."* Stéphanie Pouzin also remembers long journeys from her childhood because the computer scientist never failed to take his family with him: *"my mother used to travel with him, and she also took us with her, most of the time. This allowed my brother Remy and my sister Anne, in particular, to speak 5 languages fluently"*. The "X" engineer remembers spending a good part of his nights and weekends on the Cyclades project. *"I spent very little time with my family, even when we took a vacation together and they followed me to the USA, India, Japan, Brazil…"* However, the computer scientist does not consider this frantic pace as one of the reasons for his separation from his wife Isabelle in 1986: *"it happened many years after the end of Cyclades"*, he explains.

Anne Pouzin, 55 years old, is now a graphic designer and draftswoman. During her adolescence, in the middle of the Cyclades project, she followed her father's work with great interest and even helped him design his conference presentations. *"In the 1970s, between the ages of 7 and 15, in our family pavilion in Vaucresson, he had his office, a large room, where he tested the connections between his network and those of the English NPL and American Arpanet. To do this, he often asked us to send him emails (a long time before Internet emails) when he traveled to the United States or to London. It was at this time that he started working until 4:00 in the morning. In fact, we saw him mostly for dinner"*, she says, echoing her sister Stephanie's words. *"Despite all this hard work, the atmosphere was very relaxed, friendly and cool: he regularly invited people like Hubert Zimmermann, Jean-Louis Grangé and Michel Gien to his home for large barbecues in his garden in Vaucresson. Between 1974 and 1978, his travels became even more frequent, he was always on the move, in America and Europe. My mother often organized 'cultural' trips in parallel with his conferences—often those of IFIP—and they both traveled, leaving us with a babysitter. He would go away for several weeks or a month, only coming home to change suitcases."*

In October 1974, shortly after the IRIA seminar on networks in Darmstadt, Louis Pouzin and his team crossed the Atlantic to participate in the French

Scientific and Technical Exhibition at the Ontario Science Center in Toronto, where he demonstrated Cigale. "*All the people connected to the networks were present. There was a DGT site, on which we had worked hard to have a little corner of our own, a stand with a connection station… and very quickly, a mini coup d'état occurred*", says Bernard Nivelet, laughing. "*People who had come to see what we were doing told everyone else, and it was the Cyclades stand that filled up, instead of the DGT, because it was connected through the datagram with Rennes, Rocquencourt and the National Physical Laboratory in London. It was a very unique and extraordinary event, because we had just shown that we were able to connect a small computer in Canada, through all these interfaces, with another machine connected in the United Kingdom. It was a revolution.*"

In 1974, whereas the experimental RCP network had just been opened by the PTT, the Cyclades network was already at the top of its game. According to Alain Beltran and Pascal Griset,[45] "*thanks to its international and national readability, it was then recognized as the second current example of a general computer network (with Arpanet). From bright and studious students in the United States, the Cyclades men quickly transformed into masters on the European continent.*" The computer scientists led by Louis Pouzin, with their success, even supplanted the NPL researchers in a European computer network project designed to equal the Arpanet: the European Informatics Network (EIN). A network developed since 1973 as part of the EU's COST 11 (European Cooperation in Science and Technology) program.[46] Faced with the engineers from the United Kingdom (even though they were in charge of the project), Norway, Italy, Portugal, Yugoslavia, Switzerland and Sweden gathered for the occasion, the highly active Cyclamen took over, with their idea of independent packets, or datagrams, as well as the idea of using Mitra 15 computers from the CII—to the extent that the EIN ended up looking like a sort of European Cigale in its specifications, linking IRIA (Rocquencourt), ETH (Federal Institute of Technology Zurich), NPL (London), JRC (Joint European Research Center, Ispra, Italy) and the Milan Polytechnic School.

A newcomer was in charge of Cyclades operations within the EIN project. A 1971 graduate of the Ecole Centrale Paris, Michel Gien developed programming languages at Bull, before joining the "network team" at the University of Grenoble (which was working in conjunction with the IRIA Cyclades project), then Rocquencourt as a system engineer at the Institute's

---

[45] Alain Beltran and Pascal Griset, "Histoire d'un pionnier de l'informatique: 40 ans de recherche à l'INRIA", EDP Sciences, 2007.

[46] "L'Europe des réseaux dans les années 1970, entre coopérations et rivalités", Valérie Schafer, interstices. info, 2009, https://interstices.info/jcms/c_45877/l-europe-des-reseaux-dans-les-annees-1970-entre-cooperations-et-rivalites

computing center. There, he regularly met with the members of Cyclades: "*I came to be in contact with them because they used the same computers to develop their programs. And quite quickly I met Louis Pouzin, who was looking to bring people into his project, but who didn't necessarily have all the positions he needed. He was trying to convince people who worked in other teams to work for Cyclades*", he says.[47] Quickly, the 27-year-old computer scientist became involved in the DGI project, until he heard about the COST 11 project in 1974: "*One day, Louis called me and asked 'do you speak English?', I said 'yes', because I had been to the United States. He told me 'we're looking for someone to introduce Cyclades to the COST 11 project; come to me, I'll brief you, then you can go to the COST 11 project…' He started my career like that*", recalls the man who now runs *Twinlife*, a startup that designs mobile messaging applications to compete with *WhatsApp*.[48] Promoted to the position of technical manager for relations between the EIN and Cyclades projects, Michel Gien actively promoted datagrams and the Cigale protocol, and later followed Louis Pouzin and Hubert Zimmermann in their work within the IFIP and INWG for the standardization of protocols at international level.

Helping his men get a foot in the door: this is one of Louis Pouzin's qualities that his "disciples" most frequently cite. "*He didn't hesitate to take me, a young engineer, and to propel me into a European project with people who were twice as old and experienced! Louis often did this: he found people, launched them, found them contacts and funding. After Cyclades, in 1979, he launched spin offs, pilot projects at INRIA: he pushed Jean Le Bihan towards databases (Sirius project) for example, and he launched me on a Unix-compatible operating system project, SOL, which finally led me to co-found the startup Chorus Systems in 1986 with Hubert Zimmermann*", says Michel Gien.

The small team was further expanded in 1975, with the arrival of the Franco-Lebanese Najah Naffah at Cyclades. A doctoral student at ENST[49] (Ecole Nationale Supérieure des Télécommunications—National Higher Institution of Telecommunications), then called "Institut Télécom", who joined IRIA after working for 3 years as a civil engineer on the installation of automatic radars in Lebanon. "*I was then trying to write a thesis on connections between computers—which did not communicate with each other at the time, especially when they came from two different manufacturers. I had to connect an*

---

[47] Interview with Michel Gien, March 3, 2017.

[48] "Twinlife: WhatsApp avec l'éthique en plus", Serge Abiteboul and Marie Jung, Binaire, 5 septembre 2016, http://binaire.blog.lemonde.fr/2016/09/05/twinlife-whatsapp-avec-lethique-en-plus/

[49] NAFFAH, Najah—*Étude de la gestion des terminaux dans un réseau général informatique et développement d'un système microprogrammé pour la connexion directe d'un terminal intelligent sur le Réseau CYCLADES*. Thèse d'ingénieur-Docteur, Université Paris VI – (Fr), Dec. 1975, 237 p.

image lab with my school's computer center (ENST), and I realized that it was best to join a research group for my study. I met Louis through a common acquaintance, and he explained that he needed to connect intelligent terminals as part of his research program with IRIA. The meeting only lasted a very short time, 15 minutes, as I was busy, but I immediately started looking into it." After completing his thesis at the end of 1975, the young computer scientist officially joined Cyclades as a research engineer. At the end of the project, Louis Pouzin further entrusted him with a "spin off", a pilot project in its own right, consisting in creating the "workstation of the future": *Kayak*. "*This project, supervised by Louis, allowed me to develop a more powerful station than the Macintosh. Just as he initiated Jean-Louis Grangé's pilot project, NADIR, which consisted in creating a network through satellite systems, Louis clearly put me on track, without asking for anything in return*", recalls Najah Naffah. "*Louis Pouzin was really a motivating factor, a team leader, a driving force for his men. He was able to find the right people from his close circle of acquaintances. He set up a team with people he already knew, who were enthusiastic about the project, or, and this is his great strength, in whom he was able to recognize hidden skills*", says Valérie Schafer.

Michel Gien describes the atmosphere of his time at Cyclades with the "Pouzin gang": "*We were all bright young things, a bit hippish, and we travelled a lot—to Grenoble, Toulouse, to universities, but also to Boston, Stanford and Los Angeles. The atmosphere was very warm and motivating. We wanted to change the world, we were not afraid of anything. And between Louis Pouzin, Hubert Zimmermann, Jean-Louis Grangé, Gérard Le Lann, Jean Le Bihan, Najah Naffah and myself, we formed a solid group.*" Even today, the members of the Cyclades team continue to see each other. "*Hubert Zimmermann and Jean Le Bihan have passed away, but those who remain regularly organize meals together: the Cyclades dinners*", explains Jean-Louis Grangé. "*In the 1970s, marked by the emergence of network technologies and the 30 golden years after World War 2, we were a bunch of friends, young, enthusiastic and passionate about what we were doing. It was exciting, because we realized that it was completely new, that it was something important internationally.*"

Led by Louis Pouzin, whom his men affectionately nicknamed "Luigi", Cyclades quickly took on international dimensions: the Cyclades team set up cooperation with the NPL and Arpanet (of which a node was created in London) in 1974, in order to conduct communication experiments, and why not connect networks—Louis Pouzin being part, with Hubert Zimmermann, of the IFIP and INWG (International Network Working Group) network think tanks, and actively participating in ISO, in order to reflect on the standardization of computer architectures.[50] "*The idea was to agree on common protocols, and that's what later led the second version of TCP to be influenced by Cyclades*", explains Michel Gien.

"*There was at once a French culture in our team, with an easy welcome for foreign researchers, and a certain American culture, because we welcomed a lot of researchers from the United States, and we visited them too. We were very multi-cultural, with an atmosphere based on openness. We didn't hide our work, we were constantly communicating, exchanging, discussing freely, having a lot of fun; in the carefree 1970s, we never worked seriously, without telling jokes*", recalls Najah Naffah.

Louis Pouzin concludes: "*We all had very strong ties among ourselves in the team. It was an ambitious project. We did things that no one else had done before. I believe that what I have passed on to my men is a way of presenting things, especially in public, with conviction. And also the certainty that you shouldn't let yourself be stepped on when you're dealing with people who think what you're doing is wrong or won't work…*".

In 1974, the Cyclades project team, in addition to its "hard core" members (Hubert Zimmermann, Louis Pouzin, Michel Gien, Jean-Louis Grangé, Gérard Le Lann, Najah Naffah), was made up of university delegates, students who came to do tests, and engineers seconded by service companies—up to between 15 and 20 people.

5.4.2   1974/Pressure from PTT/Louis Pouzin, the Activist/ Fundamental Differences

When they started in 1972, Louis Pouzin and his team had everything they needed to succeed: "*the DGI had money to devote to the Cyclades project, a good scientific and technical hosting structure for the team (IRIA), strong political support, and potential industrial partners to provide computers and engineers: the CII, and engineering companies formed from major armaments programs, including the SESA SSII,[51] founded by the polytechnician Jacques Stern, who had worked 2 years earlier as an engineer in charge of air defense systems, within the Technical Service of Air Telecommunications (STTA), on the development of the computerized air monitoring system, the TRIDEN system*",[52] summarizes Pierre-Éric Mounier Kuhn.

---

[50] "The Work of IFIP Working Group 6 .1", Alex Curran and Vinton Cerf, 1975.

[51] Société d'études des systèmes d'automation—Company for the study of automation systems.

[52] "Le temps des ingénieurs de la navigation aérienne—Mémoires techniques, 1945–1985", Collection mémoire de l'aviation civile, mission mémoire de l'aviation civile, 2013.

In 1973, at the same time as the Arpanet in the United States, Louis and his men multiplied the demonstrations of Mitranet / Cigale, which was almost operational, in schools, banks, scientific and industrial circles, and before the Ministers Jean Charbonnel and Hubert Germain, who planned to create a common public network between the PTT and the "Pouzin boys". This *"arranged marriage of the telephone and the computer"*, as Valérie Schafer nicknamed it, led two very different worlds, the CNET engineers and the IRIA computer scientists, to work together, *"because computers communicate with each other through transmission lines and switching centers"*.[53]

However, there was soon a divergence in the vision of data routing in the network by the two groups of engineers. IRIA wanted to connect machines from different manufacturers, with different OS, and opted for datagrams. The CNET, which mainly thought in terms of data transport and wanted speed, chose virtual circuits. *"The PTT wrongly considered the isolated packet mode as unreliable. They also wanted to maintain their monopoly, and not give up control to specialized links"*, notes Louis Pouzin. Two opposing visions which appeared increasingly irreconcilable: that of Cyclades, which was to design a general network of computers, and that of the PTT and the Directorate-General for Telecommunications, which, because of their culture of link security and service billing, feared losing control over the network if datagrams were adopted.[54]

Given that PTT was a monopoly, the balance of power was inherently unequal, and the fragile agreement between Cyclades and the DGT was rapidly unraveling. In the spring of 1973, Louis Pouzin noted that the cooperation agreement between the two teams had not ended the CNET's parallel project, and that PTT engineers were still working on their own network. In addition, contact between the two teams was rare and happened mainly through intermediaries (Maurice Allègre from the DGI, Louis-Joseph Libois from the DGT). Everyone was therefore carrying out their own project by themselves, while trying to keep up appearances. *"The telecoms were more than cautious, they were outright hostile to the datagram solution. There was, it can be said, a real rivalry between the projects. In reality, the two teams had no desire to work together"*, says Valérie Schafer.[55] In her view, *"each team then pursued its own project, with the feeling that collaboration with the other team would be more disabling than profitable"*.

[53] "La France en réseaux", Valérie Schafer, Nuvis, 2012.
[54] "Inventing the Internet", Janet Abbate, MIT Press, Cambridge and London, 1999.
[55] Interview with Valérie Schafer, December 1, 2016.

At the same time, although he was supposed to remain on good terms with the telecom operators, Louis Pouzin was very provocative and publically voiced his disagreement with the choice of virtual circuits by the CNET. "*Louis caught everyone's attention: he published articles and moderated conferences where he didn't beat about the bush, praising his approach (datagrams) and demolishing the PTT approach rather aggressively, which didn't please them and fuelled the conflict*", recalls Najah Naffah. He remembers with amusement a paper in which Louis Pouzin praised the virtues of datagrams as opposed virtual circuits, published in the IRIA journal. "*The journal was removed as soon as it was published, and all printed copies, 4500, were immediately destroyed! At the time, we weren't supposed to attack a technology promoted by the administration, or at least not in this way*", he says with a little smile. "*Louis attacked without reservation, publicly, in front of everyone. That's his provocative side. What he said was not random: he had an idea that was worth defending. But we could have presented it with a little more tact.*"

At the DGI, Philippe Renard was also struck by this episode, the mention of which never fails to make him laugh: "*IRIA produced a bulletin every quarter, and Louis had been asked to write the introductory text in one of them, in order to present Cyclades. This led him to put forward his point of view and to make negative allusions to the DGT project... When the IRIA text arrived on the minister's desk, the people of the Hermès project complained to him that the document was publicly critical... To destroy the documents already distributed, IRIA had to race over to all the subscribing organizations. They finally managed to retrieve the incriminating publication and replaced it with one where instead of Louis' text was a more consensual one by the director André Danzin. It was pretty funny, we all had a good laugh!*"

Michel Gien still remembers the "combative" nature of his boss, which was not necessarily to everyone's taste: "*He was an activist, the fox in the chicken coop... He was visionary when he said that the future was not to be sought in telecom networks, but in computers. But you can't convince people by asking them to saw off the branch they're sitting on...*" The former engineer of the INRIA computing center, now a "serial entrepreneur",[56] appreciated the "drive" of his former boss, without, however, downplaying his diplomatic shortcomings: "*he was fearless, like all visionaries. He put people on a trajectory and trusted them. He was very quick in his judgment of people. Those who could help him to move forward, he propelled upwards. But those who got in his way were eliminated,*

[56] "Michel Gien, fondateur de Chorus Systems", INRIA.fr, 13 avril 2015; https://www.inria.fr/innovation/recherche-partenariale-transfert/30-ans-de-creation-d-entreprise/paroles-d-entrepreneurs/michel-gien-chorus-systems

sometimes brutally. He could have toned things down a bit, been more flexible, it would have been to his advantage if he had made fewer waves. But Louis describes himself as follows: he is a fighter, who likes to occupy difficult terrain, even to the point of creating conflicts himself and rushing into battle…".

The late Michel Monpetit, the Deputy Director of SESORI at IRIA, tried to channel (or at least contain)[57] this combative personality—as did the late Hubert Zimmermann, the quiet "diplomat" of Cyclades and ardent defender of an OSI architecture in seven layers within the International Organization for Standardization. But Louis Pouzin has been cultivating it since his first professional experiences at Bull and Simca. *"I'm pretty sharp, that's for sure. I've always had some pretty biting speeches. I wasn't the type to compromise, because I knew that if you compromise, you can't do what you want. Between my team and the PTT, the imbalance of power was too great. It was like David and Goliath. So, I had to be the project tough guy, period"*, he laughs. His former colleague Michel Gien opined: *"Louis is not really a person of compromise, he is a man of conflict. He has quite clear, sharp ideas. He sticks to his guns, he tries to convince, and if people don't agree, too bad for them. With regard to the PTT, it was like this: for him, they were wrong, and all they had to do was bend to his will. Like any leader, he has his proponents and detractors. People are never indifferent where he is concerned, they either think he's great or can't stand him!"* The same opinion is shared by Jean-Louis Grangé, who recalls that Louis Pouzin *"has always been a star, but with many enemies"*.

The paradox of this hard-working computer scientist is that although he is fierce when defending a project, he is an unfailingly placid person in everyday life. *"My father is a very independent person. He listens to others a lot, but he doesn't need them to keep moving forward. And even though he was very savage against the PTT, he remained a very calm and serene person. I've rarely seen him angry. For him, every problem has a solution, and if he thinks he has found it, he does everything to promote it"*, notes Stéphanie Pouzin, from her Burgundy vineyard.

At the beginning of 1974, the already very tense relations between the computer scientists of the Cyclades project at IRIA and the engineers of the Hermès project, led at the CNET by Rémi Després—a polytechnician like Louis Pouzin, but who opted for virtual circuits—took a turn for the worse. The two sides were unable to find common ground, despite further attempts

---

[57] Michel Monpetit was accidentally killed in a car accident on his way to a meeting in the provinces in 1976. A prize created in 1977 by the Academy of Sciences bears his name. It rewards a researcher or engineer for his or her work in applied mathematics or computer science.

to bring them closer together.[58] "*Politically, people considered it a bit unfortunate that France put money into two competing projects, both on experimental computer networks. It was suggested that they cooperate, and as boss of the packet switching team at Cyclades, I joined the CNET team in Issy-les-Moulineaux to carry out joint research. But it didn't last more than 2 months, because I couldn't get along with them*", says Jean-Louis Grangé. "*They were telephone operators, telecom engineers, guys who were working on the phone at the time, and I was a computer scientist. We had a diametrically opposed vision of what should be done technically. Even humanly, the atmosphere was different. Our team was a commando team, we laughed a lot, we travelled a lot, we were very friendly, a close-knit, dynamic team… and I landed in this CNET team where people were serious, typical civil servants, never joking, and I was bored… After a while, I went to Louis, and I told him: 'This is not possible, I can't work with them, the differences go too deep'. Louis was an angel, he answered me without hesitation: "All right, come back."*

More generally, tensions surrounded the question of protocols. Bernard Nivelet, the head of IRIA's computer center and IT resources, who was in charge of Cigale, remembers that in 1972, when Philippe Picard, in charge of the "teleinformatics" subdirectorate at the DGT, had agreed to "offer" lines to them, "*it was, from his point of view, to carry out technical tests, and it was out of the question that we could, on the basis of this work, develop protocols*". Because, he explains, "*the telecom operators had politically decided to build and acquire control of the protocols, in order to create their own network, RCP, the future Transpac*". According to the engineer, "*there was fundamental opposition, because the PTT wanted a closed communications policy—where no one could do without their services—while Luigi wanted an open position, with open protocols. These were two completely incompatible visions, as much so as Windows, built on proprietary protocols and programs, and Linux, where everything is open.*"

For his part, the former member of the Délégation à l'informatique, Philippe Renard, refuses to speak of a "conflict" to describe what was then at stake between the "Luigi gang" and the PTT: "*there were mainly two philosophies, two different visions. First of all, the world of Telecommunications, which considered that it was their domain to make computer networks, and which would even have liked, at a certain time, to develop computers at the CNET, and that we rely on their expertise to design what was being built at the CII… And then, the computer vision, represented by the industry and the CII, as well as by research and Cyclades.*"

---

[58] "Du projet Hermès à Transpac", Alain Profit and Philippe Picard, Entreprises et histoire, éditions SKA, 2002.

In such a context, however, confrontation was inevitable. Especially when fate got involved and hit the most important backer of the Cyclamen. On April 2, 1974, 2 months after a new presentation of Cyclades to the government,[59] Georges Pompidou died of cancer, 2 years before the end of his term in office. His Minister of Economy and Finance, the ambitious Valéry Giscard d'Estaing, waited a few days, then announced his candidacy for the presidency of the Republic. The young mayor of Chamalières became president on May 27, defeating François Mitterrand by a narrow margin, with a bare 50.81% of the votes. *"For him, the Cyclades project had no electoral interest, it was just a gadget for researchers. But we still had no idea what he was going to do with us and the Plan Calcul"*, recalls Louis Pouzin.

---

[59] On February 8, 1974, Hubert Zimmermann presented the Cyclades project to Ministers Hubert Germain and Jean Charbonnel. https://phototheque.inria.fr/phototheque/media/22919;jsessionid=F3B 294A554F8B47EA9B84B07F0681BED

6

The End of Cyclades (1980–1989)

6.1 Luigi's Gang

In 1974, the Cyclades project network moved from the "model" phase to something concrete, operational. *"Cigale then worked perfectly. But the French telecommunications administration had decided that it had no future and that everything had to be bet on RCP, the future Transpac. Although it was dedicated to data exchanges, it was more like a traditional telephone network: it made it much easier to collect taxes. Consequently, any research to develop another technology was considered inappropriate"*, writes Christian Huitema in "Et Dieu créa l'Internet"—And God created the Internet, about the end of the Cyclades project.[1] *"For the PTT, now under the supervision of the Industrial Affairs Department, the idea of the datagram itself was utterly unacceptable: with this system, there is no way to ensure that the packet has arrived at its destination. It wasn't very "clean", it was better to use circuits"*, says Louis Pouzin, shrugging his shoulders.

In addition to the PTT, the IT specialist was also under pressure from his former company, Bull, on behalf of Valéry Giscard d'Estaing: *"In the early 1970s, this company, whose computer business was sold by General Electric to Honeywell (another American company), picked up after years of poor performance. Bull's people were then well integrated into a multinational company, where they had a role, a recognized function, which was the development of medium computer ranges... and they noted with concern that part of the French market was blocked to them by the Plan Calcul, which systematically granted*

---

[1] Christian Huitema, "Et Dieu créa l'Internet", Eyrolles, 1995.

© Springer Nature Switzerland AG 2020
C. Lebrument, F. Soyez, *The Inventions of Louis Pouzin*,
https://doi.org/10.1007/978-3-030-34836-6_6

purchasing preferences in large administrations and public services to CII", says Pierre-Éric Mounier-Kuhn. *"So, from the moment Valery Giscard d'Estaing came to power, they put as much pressure on him as possible, by joining forces with one of the CII's parent companies, the CGE [General Electric Company], to put an end to Unidata. For Bull, it was a matter of life and death."* The CGE also met its own interests through this alliance. *"This company had partly financed Giscard's campaign, it seems. However, its customers included PTT. And the Unidata Consortium (created by the Délégation à l'Informatique) included the German electronics and electricity giant Siemens, its major telephone competitor. This was intolerable for them"*, says Louis Pouzin.[2]

The death of the Plan Calcul is often attributed to Valéry Giscard d'Estaing's policy. But who was actually the president who ended the Cyclades project? Valéry Giscard d'Estaing was elected to the French National Assembly in 1956 and was a delegate to the United Nations General Assembly (1956–1958). He then served as Secretary of State for Finance (1959–1962) and was appointed Minister of Finance (1962–1966) by President Charles de Gaulle. During his first term as Finance Minister, France managed to balance its budgets for the first time in 30 years. But his international economic policy—including his attempt to limit American economic influence in France—and his other conservative financial measures contributed to a recession and discredited him in the business and labor sectors; he was fired. From 1969 to 1974, he was once again Minister of Finance under President Georges Pompidou. Giscard d'Estaing was elected President in the second round of voting against left-wing candidate François Mitterrand on 19 May 1974. Unlike Charles de Gaulle and Georges Pompidou, Giscard pursued a liberal and globalist policy, convinced that "problems arise on a global scale". His diplomacy thus broke with the General's hostile diplomacy, exemplified by withdrawal from NATO and vetoing British membership to the European Community, to prevent France from being in a position of "inferiority". Giscard was aware that alongside the two superpowers America and Russia, the world scene now further housed China and Japan, the oil-producing countries and the European Community. In *"Démocratie Française"*, Valéry Giscard d'Estaing writes: *"the solution of major problems concerning world security or economic development can no longer be sought in a purely national context, but gradually interests the entire international community"*. By virtue of what he

---

[2] INRA's weekly gazette, "Code Source", celebrating the Institute's 40th anniversary in 2007, writes: "In 1975, was France's industrial policy carried out at the Ministry, rue de Grenelle, or at the headquarters of the powerful Compagnie Générale d'Electricité, rue de La Boétie? Some do not hesitate to wonder given how much sway the CGE seems to have had for more than 10 years over everything to do with high-tech industries and their development in France."

called "globalism", he wanted to be "everyone's friend", starting with the Americans.[3] He remained a staunch defender of national independence, rejected bloc politics, words for European integration (one of the notable achievements of his presidency was France's role in strengthening the European Economic Community), and for France's "influence" in the world—as the leader of the middle powers and the privileged interlocutor of the super powers; and in this sense, he no longer refused to carry out projects with the USA, and even less with private actors.

So that's why, in the meantime, the new head of state was hesitant. "*He didn't know what to think of the Unidata affair. Should this great European project be carried out or not? This was the beginning of a formidable power struggle between two sides. On the one hand, the supporters of the state-led European alliance, strengthening the ICN's resources. Among them, the Delegation for Information Technology, but also a group of senior officials and some ministers, first and foremost Jacques Chirac. On the other hand, supporters of a liberal solution consisting of merging the CII with a private group, preferably an American one. Among them were Thomson's leaders, whose enthusiasm for the Unidata project was waning by the hour, and senior officials from the Ministry of Industry and the Minister himself, Michel d'Ornano. This camp had found its champion: Jean-Pierre Brulé, Honeywell-Bull's CEO. The man's dream was to crush Unidata—a formidable competitor—and, in the process, absorb the CII…*", summarizes Tristan Gaston-Breton, business historian, in *Les Echos*.[4]

A non-gaullist, more oriented towards Atlanticism than towards European integration, Valéry Giscard d'Estaing had no interest in the Plan Calcul, and was very sensitive to the arguments of Bull, the CGE and Thomson. In May 1974, the CII and the Cigale network worked perfectly. "But with his advisers, ENA[5] graduates who were very good at drawing rectangles with arrows but knew nothing about IT, the president suddenly decided to abolish the Delegation for IT, then a little later stopped the Cyclades budget", remembers Louis Pouzin bitterly. In concrete terms, just a few weeks after the Chirac government was set up, the new Minister of Industry, Michel d'Ornano, adopted a "new industrial vision" and replaced the Délégation à l'informatique, the government agency supporting IRIA and the CII, with the "Direction des industries de l'informatique et de l'électronique"—Management of the computer and electronics industries (DIELI). Disappointed, Maurice Allègre resigned, and Jean-Claude Pelissolo, an engineer trained at the ENST

---

[3] Charles Hargrove. Valéry Giscard d'Estaing, "Politique étrangère," n°1, 1986.

[4] "Le plan Calcul, l'échec d'une ambition", Tristan Gaston-Breton, Les Echos, July 20, 2012.

[5] ENA: National School of Administration.

succeeded him. Claude Kornblum, Deputy Chief of Staff to the Minister of Industry, was in charge of considering a merger between the CII and an American computer manufacturer. IBM and Honeywell-Bull were necessarily at the top of the list.[6]

One year later, on May 20, 1975, the government officially approved Honeywell-Bull's acquisition of the CII and announced its withdrawal from Unidata. This was the end of the Plan Calcul. However, the Cyclades project had not been stopped, as the PTT continued to rent and maintain the telephone lines used by Cigale. But the engineers, who for months had been developing a promising operational network, suddenly found themselves not only without money (other than IRIA's limited funds) to finance their work, but also without any support, whether industrial or governmental. "*The PTT were kind enough not to remove the leased lines and keep them in service. It was a form of benevolent laxity: they had won, they wanted the X.25, they had it! But there was more behind this act of kindness: it allowed them to see how our system worked in order to refine their own project, which was far from complete, because it was only operational four years later in 1978*", says Louis Pouzin.

For Tristan Gaston-Breton, Bull's victory was partly ideological: "*In the entourage of Valéry Giscard d'Estaing, many people believed that it was no longer a time to strengthen the public sector, even within a European framework. Liberals at heart, they believed that the priority was to strengthen private companies. Technically, an alliance between the CII and the American Honeywell-Bull seemed much more viable to them than a major European alliance*". It also confirms in passing that "*the attitude of French industrialists (CGE and Thomson-CSF) proved to be decisive*". They were "*committed to an international development strategy*", and therefore no longer wished "*to participate in an adventure born under the leadership of the State*". These same manufacturers would also have preferred, explains Louis Pouzin, "*to work with the PTT rather than with us, because it was for them a "guarantee of services", as they liked to repeat*".

"*It was David against Goliath. There was an unequal balance of power. On the one hand, you had the CNET men, who had all the means at their disposal following the implementation of a telecom catch-up plan (prepared since 1967 and adopted in 1975), and who were supported by the Ministry of PTT, with ever more funds and favors from the State to develop their digital network. And on the other hand, you had a team of computer scientists, deprived of budget, essentially developing a research network… while the telecom engineers were trying to create a network that would serve everyone—the researchers, as well as you and me,*

---

[6] Alain Beltran and Pascal Griset, "Histoire d'un pionnier de l'informatique: 40 ans de recherche à l'INRIA", EDP Sciences, 2007.

which resulted in a Minitel in every home.[7] From 1975–1976, it became quite clear that the Telecom people would win the battle", Pierre-Éric Mounier-Kuhn asserts uncompromisingly.

On the sly, without support or budget, but using the PTT lines, Louis Pouzin and his team continued their work. Between 1975 and 1978, Cigale thus continued to be operated by the IRIA computing center and used by university centers as a "test bench for future distributed computing".[8] Louis Pouzin continued to work night and day, to the delight of his children, who loved to spy on him and observe him working. "*He was experimenting with American friends, like Professor Corbató. It was late at night, and those words that were displayed on a computer screen without anyone typing on a keyboard had a magical side*", recalls his daughter Stephanie, who was 6 years old in 1976. "*Although Cyclades no longer officially existed as a project, and although I received a letter from André Danzin, the director of IRIA, telling me that I should no longer deal with networks… I kept doing it. He knew very well that I would not follow the directives in his letter, written by order of the ministry, and he let me do what I wanted*", says Louis Pouzin. "*Then, little by little, each university center participating in Cyclades finally moved on to something else. In the absence of funding and support, the project petered out, until it was disconnected in 1978.*"

According to Pierre-Éric Mounier-Kuhn, who takes an objective historian's look at the last years of Cyclades, "*we could have imagined a government that was broadminded enough, generous enough and had sufficiently long-term views to keep this project in the form of a technology watch team, and a network that would have continued to serve universities—with an international dimension, since it was connected to NPL Net and to a European network created at the same time. But there was a real desire on the part of the DGT to kill this competitor.*" And while Louis Pouzin, "*who had convictions well rooted in the validity of his research*", was scrambling to explain to the scientific community that Cyclades and datagram networks were the future, "*he was told that the RCP/Transpac network, and more broadly the networks based on the X.25 standard, were already being implemented, and that this was the future. Because these virtual circuit networks were then the only types of digital networks where the problem of invoicing, and therefore profitability, and also security, had been solved.*" However,

---

[7] The Minitel was a Videotex online service accessible through telephone lines, and is considered one of the world's most successful pre-World Wide Web online services. The service was introduced commercially throughout France in 1982 by the PTT. From its early days, users could make online purchases, train reservations, check stock prices, search the telephone directory, receive mail, and chat in a similar way to what is now made possible by the Internet. Technically, Minitel refers to the terminals, while the network is known as Télétel. https://www.minitel.org/

[8] "La France en réseaux", Valérie Schafer, Nuvis, 2012.

notes the CNRS researcher, "*in 1975–1976, the commercial potential of Cyclades, or Arpanet in the United States, was non-existent: it was a very interesting tool to share files, to exchange on databases, to send e-mails between researchers and academics, but no one was using it for commercial purposes*".

During the 3 years when Cyclades was continuing in secret, as best as they could, the CNET engineers continued to develop their own network, based on virtual circuits, RCP. In September 1976, the International Telegraph and Telephone Consultative Committee (CCITT),[9] the telecommunications standards body, issued a "recommendation" and established the X.25 standard—a protocol originally designed for Datapac in Canada, and for Tymnet and Telenet in the United States, but very similar to, or even strongly inspired by the RCP network—as the standard to be followed for packet switched networks.[10] Even though this was only a recommendation, the Cyclades project, based on datagrams, was increasingly isolated. "*With the X.25 standard, European and American telephone operators agreed on a way to transmit information packets, which consisted in sending packets in a row on virtual circuits... It was the triumph of the PTT*", explains Louis Pouzin bitterly. According to his sidekick Jean-Louis Grangé, "*when CCITT decreed that this protocol was the norm, it was a turning point, the beginning of the end for us. It was the beginning of something totally contrary to what we were developing, because it meant that all manufacturers, all public networks would be based on virtual circuits.*"

On December 14, 1978, the PTT moved to the next stage of their project, which no longer had any competitors: RCP officially became Transpac, the "first commercial network" for "packet data transmission" in France, and its protocol was based entirely on the X.25 standard. It is this network, initially intended for professionals, which was eventually used by the PTT in 1982 to operate the Minitel system (the Transpac/Télétel network) and its consumer services. As Julien Mailland, assistant professor in telecommunications at Indiana University Media School, explains in *The Atlantic*, "*in 1991, most Americans had not yet heard of the internet. But all of France was online, buying, selling, gaming, and chatting, thanks to a ubiquitous little box that connected to the telephone. It was called Minitel. It was a computer terminal. It housed a screen, a keyboard, and a modem—but not a microprocessor. Instead of computing on its own, Minitel connected to remote services via uplink, like a 1960s mainframe or a modern Google Chromebook. Terminals were given out, for free, to every French telephone subscriber by the state (which also ran the phone*

[9] Today, the International Telecommunication Union (ITU).
[10] "Internationalizing the Internet: The Co-evolution of Influence and Technology", Byung-Keun Kim, Edward Elgar Publishing, 2005.

company)."[11] He also observes that the "*Minitel was a huge success. With free terminals at home or work, people in France could connect to more than 25,000 online services long before the world wide web had even been invented. Many services of the dotcom-and-app eras had precursors in 1980s France. With a Minitel, one could read the news, engage in multi-player interactive gaming, grocery shop for same-day delivery, submit natural language requests like 'reserve theater tickets in Paris', purchase said tickets using a credit card, remotely control thermostats and other home appliances, manage a bank account, chat, and date.*"[12]

What was the atmosphere like when Cyclades came to an end? No anger, no sadness, just great disappointment, and a huge mess to be cleaned up. Pierre-Éric Mounier-Kuhn describes it: "*It discouraged many people, they were disgusted. The politicians who supported the Plan Calcul, the people at the CII, the researchers of the IRIA, the partner companies, the organizations that used the Cigale network… No one understood Valéry Giscard d'Estaing's change of position.*" According to the IT historian, "*this has cost the French a lot of money, it also greatly damaged their reputation in the eyes of Unidata's German and Dutch partners*". Thus, the shutting down of Cyclades and the CII by the Giscard-Chirac duo "*strengthened the stereotypes held by the engineers at Philips and Siemens, who participated in Unidata, that the French were fickle, unreliable, would say one thing and do another…*" With a lasting effect. "*For at least 10 years, when French people—in IT but also in other sectors—suggested collaborations with German or Dutch companies, they were told, with an ironic smile, that if it was to end up like Unidata, no thanks. It cost a lot of money in terms of contracts and reputation, and reputation is a long-term phenomenon…*".

According to Pierre-Éric Mounier-Kuhn, the political decision to end Cyclades even led to a kind of brain drain. "*The CII executives and engineers were incredibly invested in this project, they spent their days and nights, as well as their weekends, working to develop computers and to build Unidata, in sometimes difficult negotiations with the Germans and the Dutch… And we broke them. Suddenly, people who had acquired skills were pushed out, and they were disgusted. This was the opposite effect of the one expected, since this had all started with a desire to modernize France…*".

Thinking back to the end of Cyclades, Najah Naffah shakes his head: "*A project must always come to an end at some point. However, project results must be leveraged… It was not a sudden stop, what we should have done was to try to*

---

[11] "Minitel, the Open Network Before the Internet", Julien Mailland, The Atlantic, June 16, 2017. https://www.theatlantic.com/technology/archive/2017/06/minitel/530646/

[12] "Minitel: Welcome to the Internet", Julien Mailland et Kevin Driscoll, MIT Press, 2017. https://mit-press.mit.edu/books/minitel

implement processes to industrialize the results of our research… We could have done more for commercial successes than we did." Which was not surprising: according to Valérie Schafer, the Cyclades team was characterized by a "researcher mindset", closer to the Arpanet team than to the team that developed the RCP/Transpac network. Their goal was above all to innovate and design an effective tool rather than "to define uses, especially commercial ones".

Why, when the Cyclades projects in France and Arpanet in the USA were so similar at that time, did one of them continue until the Internet was born, while the other, which promised to form the basis of a real European computer network, was completely squashed? According to Michel Gien, the American researchers had a major advantage: they were funded by a national heavyweight, the ARPA, with "firm" objectives and a clearly defined vision. In parallel, Anglo-American scientists were supported by Bolt, Beranek and Newman (BBN), as well as by prestigious universities (UCLA, Stanford Research Institute, University of California at Santa Barbara*). "They were able to get their protocol implemented quickly… While Cyclades was a much more collaborative project, suffering from political quarrels (IT versus telcos). The idea in France was: 'we standardize, we discuss matters in international standardization bodies, we try to reach an agreement with the PTT'; whereas in the United States it was, 'we implement, it then becomes a standard, then everyone copies us! This operating mode had a much greater impact than ours…. Even though the work of the Arpanet team continued for several years longer and, it can be said, our work had a certain degree of influence on their protocols and technical choices, especially for the second version of TCP".*

According to Twinlife's CEO, "*the difference with the Americans is that, in France, we developed a whole range of skills, but we never really managed to convince users (large companies, consumers) to use what we created. We were a little ahead of the market, which was almost non-existent in Europe, whereas in the USA, the market was already there… The United States had a single market, strong political will, and the industrial vision of ARPA that provided the necessary means to develop it nationally and then internationally. In France, it was impossible. The context (a very strong telco culture) did not allow you in France, and in Europe, to succeed as compared to the United States, we were just little mice.*"

Pierre-Eric Mounier-Kuhn confirms the difference in scale between the French and American projects: "*In the USA, there were already many extensions of networks of this type: Arpanet had widely expanded, with network nodes multiplying, and had given demos at major shows (such as the Computer Fair in the USA in 1973 and 1974, with a demonstration of exchanges with Cyclades in France and the NPL in the UK), which had convinced manufacturers*". The historian goes back to the origin of the Internet, which could have been the genesis of the "Catenet" imagined by Louis Pouzin in 1972: "*At the beginning of the 1980s, there was the decisive decision by the American Defense department to divide Arpanet in two, between a civil network to serve universities and a strictly military, independent network. The purely civil network was made available to academics and the entire—Net ecosystem that existed in the USA at the time (Ethernet, CSNET, BITNET and Usenet, networks developed by universities that were not linked to ARPA, but which had the same model as Arpanet, with packet and datagram switching). It was then taken over by American commercial companies, which began to develop sales and advertising systems. And then all these inter-researcher communication networks, Arpanet and its clones, were linked within a single "network of networks", making it possible in 1993 to open the Internet to commercial interests*".

In France, resentment was strong in the 1980s, because the worlds of the members of the Cyclades project and those of the Hermès/Transpac project were not so distant, at the outset. "*These were two worlds which knew each other well (at the DGI, my boss, Alain Profit, came from the CNET and the telecom sector; there was continuous to and fro between these two worlds), and the Cyclades project in any case was not intended to be a product made available to a telecommunications clientele: that was the DGT's role*", Philippe Renard explains. But between 1976 and 1978, the year Cyclades was shut down, clashes between technicians became ever more intense, to the point of definitively burying any hope of reconciliation. During the period when Cigale continued to operate, but without a budget, Louis Pouzin made full use of his network of professionals to defend and promote internationally his vision of a communication system based on datagrams, and to publicly oppose that of the CNET and the Telecommunications Administration. Thanks to these actions, the balance of power was slightly leveled. "*He had a very wide audience (because many countries were beginning to take an interest in computer networks), through meetings within the context of the IFIP, which Rémi Després did not have. This international IT organization played a very important role in the field by bringing together the specialists of the time, and he led the network working group there. Louis had, in the international field, technologically surpassed the technical vision of the PTT*", recalls Philippe Renard.

The engineer at the head of Cyclades was so militant and adamant when he tried to convey his ideas that, in the summer of 1976, André Danzin even intervened in person to defend "the necessary cordial understanding" between IRIA and the PTT, even if it was then only on paper. In early August,[13] at the

---

[13] At the same time, Bernard Nivelet, who had left for Cyclades in the USA, was urgently called back to IRIA following a "serious air conditioning accident", which caused a "dust cloud" that had covered the engine room of the Computer Center.

ICCC (International Conference on Computer Communication) in Toronto—the city where, 2 years earlier, he had made a flamboyant demonstration of Cigale— Louis Pouzin directly criticized virtual circuits. While CCETT and CNET were presenting a functional X.25 software prototype (1 month before the CCITT's decisive opinion on this protocol) and were demonstrating the experimental network RCP,[14] the Cyclades team carried out, for the duration of the congress, their own Cigale demos. Louis Pouzin spoke at a parallel conference and did not hesitate to accuse the PTT, explains Valérie Schafer in *"La France en réseaux"*,[15] of having *"signed a pact to refuse datagrams, even though they are simpler than virtual circuits"*, in order to *"get out of their role as bit carriers, to capture the market, and to make users hostage to their technical choices and standards"*.

The computer scientist's fiery intervention[16] (in his eyes, purely scientific) disturbed the representatives of IRIA, DIELI and DGT, who considered it dangerous for France's image and industrial policy. *"In any case, I would rather ascribe to confusion, for which I would be responsible, the difficulties arising from your speech in Toronto where you were the IFIP guest speaker.[17] This speech, of a political nature, had the effect of fueling a controversy between PTT and ourselves, and, consequently, between the DGT and our tutelary ministry.[18] This controversy is harmful to our IT interests, because it leads to non-constructive dialogue. Of course, the press was only too happy to dramatize the debate"*, André Danzin reminded Louis Pouzin a year later.[19] But the engineer's interventions to defend datagrams bore fruit, even years after the end of his project—his research being taken up in the 1980s by Vinton Cerf and Bob Kahn for their own work, as part of Arpanet and the development of the TCP/IP protocol. While Cyclades lost the political battle, it seems to have won the battle of minds in the end.

---

[14] http://a3c7.fr/w/index.php5?title=SICOB_1976
[15] "La France en réseaux", Valérie Schafer, Nuvis, 2012.
[16] POUZIN, Louis—*The network business, Monopolies and entrepreneurs*. ICCC 76, Toronto (Ca.), Aug. 1976, p. 563–567.
[17] IFIP is the organizer of the International Conference on Computer Communication.
[18] The Ministry of Industry.
[19] Letter from André Danzin to Louis Pouzin, October 25, 1977.

6.1.1 The Impact in France and on the Internet/Arpanet II and TCP/IP

In January 1978, after the Cigale network had been disconnected and the Cyclades project definitively buried, the French Inspectorate-General of Finance published a study that disowned the work of Louis Pouzin and his team, by simply ignoring it.[20] In their famous 125-page report on "the computerization of society", which prefigured the launch of the Minitel network, Simon Nora and Alain Minc[21] explored, at the request of Valéry Giscard d'Estaing, ways to *"develop the use of information technology by the French"* in a context of economic crisis.[22] According to senior officials, as they witnessed the "rise" of what they called "telematics" (or "the growing intertwining of computers and telecommunications"), and the fact that this new sector represented for the country a "growth" and "sovereignty" issue, consumer electronics remained "underdeveloped" in France despite the Plan Calcul, the creation of the CII, and Unidata. In fact, according to them, France was "relatively absent" from the scene of "large-scale computing", and their hopes rested on the DGT's Transpac project (strengthened by the adoption of the X.25 protocol in 1976 by the CCITT), *"for the standardization of data transmission"*, as well as on the work of the CNET, *"an organization that will be a key player in future developments"*.

The field was finally clear for the Transpac network, which supplied the Minitel (under the name Télétel network) in the 1980s. *"Today,* laughs Louis Pouzin, *the X.25 protocol and the Minitel are both museum pieces!"* But even if, Jean-Louis Grangé also argues, *"Cyclades had its revenge years later when the X.25 and Minitel disappeared"*, at that time, in 1978, there was a great deal of bitterness. *"I had been called by André Danzin, Director of IRIA, to be part of the IRIA Operations Center. And it was in this context that I once witnessed a scene between Jacques Dondoux (former director of the CNET and Inspector General of the PTT), who was part of this group, and André Danzin. The former director of production at the DGT (between 1974 and 1975) told the head of the IRIA: 'You have to choose: either you stop the work with Mr. Pouzin and I help you to finance your work on communication using Transpac, or you continue and I do not guarantee a bright future for your center'. It was very simple. Danzin finally gave in, and after Cigale's extinction, Louis found himself with little or*

---

[20] Rapport Nora-Minc sur l'informatisation de la société, La documentation française, 1978. http://www.ladocumentationfrancaise.fr/rapports-publics/154000252/index.shtml

[21] He became the CFO of CII-Honeywell-Bull in 1981.

[22] "Le rapport Nora-Minc. Histoire d'un best-seller", Andrée Walliser, revue "Vingtième Siècle", n°23, July–September 1989.

nothing to do. He suffered immensely. He had been neutralized by the DGT", recalls Bernard Nivelet. According to the former head of the IRIA computing center, who became Bull France's technical director in 1984, "*the DGT's attitude has caused us to lose about 15 years of industrial expertise. Because with Louis Pouzin's work, we were able to build a computer connection as early as 1973–1974…*".

In its "Code Source" gazette, published in 2007, INRIA recalls Louis Pouzin's "humble" attitude following the final demise of his project: "*he had too much elegance to visibly show the disappointment he felt at the abandonment of Cyclades. This decision could appear all the crueller since it was in a hurry that he had accepted, at the request of the DGI, to leave Chrysler to develop a French computer network as quickly as possible. Because Pouzin was undoubtedly the right man for the job, an engineer who was very familiar with what was being done in the United States and in tune with the real needs of users. The success of Cyclades owed much to the qualities of the researcher but also to his way of creating the essential dynamics around him for a project involving actors from different backgrounds. All qualities that have not, however, preserved him from the hegemonic desires of the DGT.*"[23]

After Cigale's disconnection, the computer scientist, a little depressed, did not waste too much time lamenting his fate and quickly looked for new fields of research on which to work. "*Of course, I was angry to see Cyclades stop, but in life, all projects have an end. So, I did something else. I continued to deal with networks, of course, but not officially*", says the old man. As director of pilot projects at IRIA, Louis Pouzin supervised research projects that no longer had much to do with networks. He managed from Afar a robotics project, Spartacus, designed to help quadriplegics by allowing them to "control a robot that is able to pick up the phone". Rémy Pouzin, 17 years old at the time, remembers this robotic hand capable of grabbing a glass of water from a table without crushing it: "*compared to what we are capable of doing today, it's ridiculous, but at that time, in Rocquencourt, it was revolutionary, the future was within reach*". His father also launched a distributed database project at IRIA, as well as a project to rewrite Unix in the Pascal language rather than C, SOL, which he entrusted to Michel Gien to manage. Finally, he also asked the young Najah Naffah to think about the "office computer of the future", through the KAYAK project.

In 1980, IRIA became INRIA (Institut National de Recherche en Informatique et en Automatique—National research institute for computer

---

[23] "Code Source", "L'hebdomadaire des 40 ans de l'INRIA", "Louis Pouzin: le cœur de Cyclades", March 2017, p. 21.

science and automation).[24] The Ministry of Industry then created the Agence pour l'informatique (ADI—Computer Agency),[25] with the idea that "*we, the former IRIA network teams, could do something else and work on applications*". The vocation of the ADI was to "promote new uses of information technology in France (in the private sector) and research oriented towards these uses". The Cyclades team, for its part, had been entirely and definitively dismantled: "*Almost all my staff had been taken from me and distributed throughout the ADI. All INRIA had left were math students*", says Louis Pouzin, who refused to join the ADI despite many requests. "*The president of the agency, Bernard Lorimy, had suggested that I come with him to lead pilot projects. But in reality, it was mainly to manage files. I wasn't interested. I considered that this agency had been created mainly for marketing purposes, to encourage administrations and France to move towards computer technologies, which were obviously not very advanced at the time*", recalls the computer scientist.

6.2   From CNET to TC6

With Hubert Zimmermann, he chose to offer his services to the CNET. "*I contacted its director, Maurice Bernard, whom I knew well, and then I went over to the enemy!*", he laughs. "*The Telecom laboratory, which created the X.25 standard, hired us because they also wanted to conduct pilot projects*". But less than a year later, there was a change of leadership and policy: "*Maurice Bernard was replaced by Jean-Pierre Poitevin, a real apparatchik, who blocked almost all projects because of his very hierarchical vision of things*". Frustrated, Louis Pouzin nevertheless remained at the CNET, in a large office in Issy-les-Moulineaux. "*He was bored to death, especially since the IFIP conferences were losing momentum*", recalls Anne, his daughter, who was 18 at the time. To overcome the boredom and continue to work in the field of networks, Louis changed hats internally: on behalf of the CNET, he worked with ETSI, the European Telecommunications Standards Institute, to develop European standardization in computing. With Hubert Zimmermann, he defended the seven-layer OSI communication model. However, this theoretical model did not succeed

---

[24] Decree No. 79-1158 of 27 December 1979—"Création d'un institut national de recherches en informatique et en automatique (INRIA), établissement public à caractère administratif, placé sous la tutelle du ministre de l'industrie" https://www.legifrance.gouv.fr/affichTexte.do?cidTexte=JORFT EXT000000519325

[25] "L'agence de l'informatique entend être essentiellement au service des utilisateurs", Le Monde, 5 February, 1981.

in making a breakthrough "because it was too ambitious" and was replaced in 1983 by the four-layer TCP/IP model.

6.3   Professor-Manager at Theseus

In 1989 (at the same time the United States decided to open up the Internet to commerce), after several years of boredom at CNET, the computer scientist joined Theseus, a management school for engineers, in Sofia Antipolis, near Nice, in the south of France. For 4 years he taught computer and network technology. "*He regained his strength and reactivated his network. Certainly, he had not lost his contacts when he was at the CNET, but he did not do very interesting work at the time. The period 1980–1989 was quite sad, he had withdrawn a little bit and it was quite tense at home. So, with Theseus, things started to get a little more fun again*", says Anne Pouzin. In 1993, her father retired at the age of 62. A "retreat" that only lasted 7 years, when he started focusing on networks again, and more specifically on Internet governance.

6.4   The Life of the Datagram After Cyclades

Although the Cyclades project was definitively stopped in 1978 with the disconnection of the Cyclades network, the work of Louis Pouzin and his associates did not lie useless at the bottom of a drawer. "*The death of Cyclades did not lead to the end of the datagram. It was simply taken over by others, under a different name: TCP/IP, a protocol upon which is based a "network of networks" similar to the Catenet that I imagined in 1972: The Internet*", explains Louis Pouzin. This suite of protocols, designed for Arpanet and the basis of the Internet, was "*strongly inspired by, not to say a copy of*" OSI's "*network*" and "*transport*" layers, "*and takes up the choice of Cyclades datagrams*", he notes.

From the very beginning of the Cyclades project, there were strong ties and much exchange of knowledge with American scientists. "*We shared information, no one held any back at that time. Arpanet researchers networked for them, we networked for us, there was no competition. One mustn't forget that we had a project to link Cyclades and Arpanet!*" In August and October 1974, just before the Cyclades project was torpedoed with the end of the Plan Calcul, the "Luigi gang" carried out demonstrations of their network at the ICCC in Stockholm and at the French Scientific and Technical Exhibition in Toronto. Louis Pouzin had also published several articles on the datagram. "*I also met many European and American researchers in the IFIP Data Communications*

Committee, which I participated in… and most Americans told me that the datagram was 'much better' than virtual networks and the first version of Arpanet", he says.

Between 1973 and 1974, Vinton Cerf, a 31-year-old Stanford professor, and Robert Elliot Kahn, 36, an engineer in charge of studies on the architecture of the Arpanet network for DARPA, worked on a packet exchange network protocol, capable of replacing the "host-to-host" communication protocol NCP (Network Control Program), used until then by Arpanet and considered too "primitive", in order to create a "network of networks", called "the internetwork",[26] then "the Internet"[27]—a concept very similar to Louis Pouzin's Catenet.[28] *"I met Cerf and Kahn very often at various congresses, especially those organized by IFIP. A small mafia of network building researchers was beginning to emerge, we cooperated easily, there was no competition. We shared everything. The idea was not to keep ideas to yourself: in research, if you don't share, you fall behind"*, explains Louis Pouzin. The computer scientist laughs: *"At the time, we were all copying each other. Cyclades engineers borrowed stuff from American Arpanet researchers who in turn took stuff from us. I always told my guys: Make people steal from you, because the thieves are at least six months behind. But this time, Cyclades having been shut down by the PTT, the field was clear for those who would resume our work"*.

Initially, Arpanet had chosen a "hybrid" system, between datagrams and virtual circuits, the NPC (Network Control Program) host-to-host protocol ensuring the management of the "data transport" layer (the communication flows of the network computers and their coherence). But when Vinton Cerf and Bob Kahn finally drew the outlines of the future TCP/IP protocol in the summer of 1973, they chose the "pure datagrams" solution. The flows were no longer controlled by the network via a communication circuit, but by the machines themselves, the data being encapsulated in datagrams. Following

---

[26] "A Protocol for Packet Network Intercommunication", IEEE, May 1974. http://www.cs.princeton.edu/courses/archive/fall06/cos561/papers/cerf74.pdf

[27] https://www.livinginternet.com/i/ii_cerf.htm

[28] In July 1978, when Vinton Cerf developed the TCP/IP protocol that serves as the basis for the Internet, he documented the project in document IEN 48, referring to "The catenet model for internetworking". https://www.rfc-editor.org/ien/ien48.txt

He writes in the introduction: "The term "catenet" was introduced by L. Pouzin in 1974 in his early paper on packet network interconnection". The document in question is dated May 1974: "A Proposal for Interconnecting Packet Switching Networks", L. Pouzin, Proceedings of EUROCOMP, Bronel University.   https://books.google.fr/books/about/A_Proposal_for_Interconnecting_Packet_Sw. html?id=VYr1tgAACAAJ&redir_esc=y

It was in preparation for the conference (at the Eurocomp) from which this paper was drawn that Louis Pouzin first described the Catenet—in March 1974, in document INWG60.

their work,[29] officially published in May 1974,[30] DARPA, Stanford researchers and BBN established three TCP/IP networks between 1975 and 1983, the year in which NCP was declared obsolete and Arpanet adopted this new protocol exclusively.[31]

What was Cyclades' contribution in this context? Did Louis Pouzin (and his team) play a role, even indirectly, in the creation of the Internet? The question is obviously a thorny one, since each stakeholder has their own version. Net historians prefer to see the history of the "network of networks" as a collective adventure, bringing together teams of researchers from all over the world, not just a handful of people. "*There is no single inventor of the Internet, there is no 'origin' of the Internet. Above all, there is a combination between the spirit of the times, a multitude of innovations, as well as favorable political and geopolitical contexts; which means that at one point, everything converged, not without difficulties*", explains Valérie Schafer. According to her, power struggles took place in the 1970s, "*in France between the PTT and Cyclades, but also in international arenas… and at the very heart of the Arpanet project with tensions within the discussions around TCP/IP and protocols*". Thus, with regard to the standardization of computer system communications, Hubert Zimmermann and Louis Pouzin "*had allies in international discussions, but Bob Kahn was firmly against them*", he refused to "adapt" the OSI (rejected by the CCITT in favor of the X.25) for the Internet model—an option that his colleague Vint Cerf, who had worked on the design of this seven-layer architecture at the INWG between 1972 and 1975 with Louis Pouzin, Hubert Zimmermann, Alex McKenzie and Donald Davies, was, in contrast, happy to defend.[32]

Is Louis Pouzin one of the "Fathers of the Internet", as the organizers of the Queen Elizabeth Prize for Engineering, awarded to the computer scientist in June 2013 at Buckingham Palace, have called him?[33] "*In history, we have completely given up the idea that there was a single inventor of the Internet. Is its history limited to the creation of TCP/IP, or is it a series of innovations that ultimately lead to the interconnection of networks? If one considers that there are 'founding fathers', then yes, Louis Pouzin is part of this story—alongside a few dozen other pioneers*", says Valérie Schafer. According to her, the work of the

---

[29] http://histoire-internet.vincaria.net/public/archives/rfc675.pdf

[30] https://ieeexplore.ieee.org/document/1092259/?tp=&arnumber=1092259

[31] http://histoire-internet.vincaria.net/post/histoire/internet/1974/TCP-IP

[32] "OSI: The Internet That Wasn't", Andrew L. Russell, IEEE Spectrum. https://spectrum.ieee.org/tech-history/cyberspace/osi-the-internet-that-wasnt

[33] "Louis Pouzin, pionnier de l'Internet", Éric Albert, July 2, 2013, Le Monde. https://abonnes.lemonde.fr/technologies/article/2013/07/01/louis-pouzin-pionnier-de-l-internet_3439915_651865.html

engineer and his team "*certainly made France part of the history of data and Internet networks and has helped to ensure that we have a history of the Internet that also has its roots in Europe. Because there are European contributions to this history of the Internet, and Cyclades played a major role in this.*"

Although in 1972, at the beginning of the Cyclades project, French researchers drew inspiration from what was being done in the United States, particularly at BBN and within the scope of Arpanet, Louis Pouzin and his men rapidly developed their own system, seeking, as Valérie Schafer notes, "*to correct weaknesses detected in the American network*". The Cyclades and Arpanet teams exchanged ideas quite regularly, cooperation having been initiated in 1972 between IRIA, Arpa and BBN, in the form of contracts. In addition to the "loan" of Gérard Le Lann to Vint Cerf in 1973, one notes the arrival in France of a BBN consulting engineer in 1972 (who gave his opinion on Cigale), and the visit of Louis Pouzin to BBN in Cambridge, near his former MIT lab, in 1975—where, while Cyclades was at a standstill, the French IT specialist was busy examining "maintenance and security issues" in the Arpa network. "*The French and Americans also met at the INWG, which played a role in "pre-standardization" and injection of proposals to ISO*", adds Valérie Schafer in her doctoral thesis.

Vinton Cerf, co-creator of the TCP/IP protocol with Robert Kahn, frequently cites Louis Pouzin, calling him the "datagram guru", as one of his key influences. It was by listening to the French researcher "*speak, very clearly, about the need to have pure datagram systems, and not virtual circuits*" at the INWG Network Working Group and the IFIP Protocol Group (which he chaired between 1973 and 1975),[34] that Vinton Cerf eventually came to choose the first option.[35] In an article published in "*Libération*" in 1998, entitled "Et la France ne créa pas l'Internet" (And France did not create the Internet) he states in particular: "*Pouzin's work has brought us a lot. We used its flow control system for the TCP/IP protocol. It was motivating to talk to him.*"[36] Furthermore, the designers of the Internet-based protocol also adopted the concept of "sliding windows" designed for Cyclades by Gérard Le Lann in Rennes in 1972. "*TCP's sliding window flow control, which allows flow control, is the direct result of discussions with Louis Pouzin and Gérard Le Lann. In fact, the latter came to Stanford University in 1974 and participated in many projects*

---

[34] "The Work of IFIP Working Group 6 .1", Alex Curran and Vinton Cerf, 1975.

[35] "Oral History of Vinton (Vint) Cerf", interviewed by Donald Nielson, November 7, 2007, Computer History Museum/ http://archive.computerhistory.org/resources/access/text/2012/04/102658186-05-01-acc.pdf

[36] "Et la France ne créa pas l'Internet—récit d'un beau gâchis", Laurent Mauriac and Emmanuèle Peyret, March 27, 1998, Libération.

with me, and I remember an evening when Bob Metcalfe, Le Lann and I were sitting in the living room of my house in Palo Alto, facing a whiteboard, trying to sketch TCP state diagrams", said Vint Cerf to Donald Nielson of the Computer History Museum in Mountain View in 2007.[37]

Robert Kahn, on the other hand, has a rather distant attitude towards the work of Louis Pouzin and the Cyclades team. Unlike Vinton Cerf, the computer scientist at Darpa and BBN did not work directly with the French engineer, and although the relations between the two former network professionals are cordial, each has a different version of what happened in 1974. "Professor Kahn" recognizes the work of the Cyclades project: "*Louis Pouzin is one of the pioneers in the field of networks. The Arpanet project had existed since the 1960s, but the Cyclades project was unique because of its work on the notion of communication via pure datagrams. A decentralized mechanism, never before seen. But unlike us in the USA, where we had the support of our government and Darpa, Pouzin's work at IRIA was not universally supported in France, it was hindered by the French PTT, and he could not really complete his research, which was really decisive.*"[38] The co-creator of TCP/IP admits that, "*unlike Vint, I had little contact with Louis Pouzin, and therefore had very little knowledge, during the work on the second version of the Arpanet protocol, of what he was doing in France*". According to him, "*the majority of our work is not related to Louis Pouzin's studies*". But he points out, however, that "*Vint has a different opinion*" from his own... Kahn further states, "*I consider Louis as a good friend. I have always been impressed by his work. He is determined, conscientious, ingenious, he showed great resilience during Cyclades, and the prototype he built has largely fed the research community. Cigale was one of the examples of a network on which to draw inspiration—but it was not the only one, because at the beginning of the 1970s, there was also the Arpanet, and the NPL*".

For Gérard Le Lann, there is no doubt on the question, given the meetings between French and American researchers, and in particular his visit to Stanford between May 1973 and June 1974. As Valérie Schafer notes: "*the French contributed to the birth of the notion of pure datagrams*".[39] According to Le Lann, "*it is in the Cyclades docs that for the first time one finds a very clear distinction between packet flows and isolated packets, or datagrams*", and "*the contributions of the IRIA project to the genesis of TCP also show this distinction,*

[37] "Oral History of Vinton (Vint) Cerf", interviewed by Donald Nielson, 7 November, 2007. http://archive.computerhistory.org/resources/access/text/2012/04/102658186-05-01-acc.pdf

[38] Interview with Bob Kahn, 5 January, 2017.

[39] "The Cyclades and Internet network: what opportunities for France in the 1970s?", Valérie Schafer, CHEFF, séminaire Haute Technologie, March 14, 2007, https://www.economie.gouv.fr/files/schafer-reseau-cyclades.pdf

which did not initially exist in Arpanet, between individual packets and message flows (between "datagrams" and "virtual circuits"). Moreover, the contribution of Cyclades is recognized by Vinton Cerf and Robert Kahn: the work carried out by the Arpanet community irrefutably integrates concepts that came from our research, and this is stated clearly in the founding paper on TCP[40,41]: *Arpanet researchers recognize that they have taken up the clear distinction of the isolated packet, as well as the mechanism of virtual windows. Cyclades was therefore useful, necessary, and played an influential role in the rise of the Internet, notably through the precise specification of the notion of datagram and the mechanism of sliding windows".* But this former member of the Cyclades project refuses to recognize Louis Pouzin as the inventor, or at least the only inventor, of the datagram. "*All this work was collective, carried out by a group of engineers, and there is not 'one' inventor for each of the innovations of that time. If we think of the Internet, we could even say that without us, without me, Louis Pouzin, Bob Kahn and Vinton Cerf, this network would still exist, because the idea (to offer something other than a file transfer service) was in the air.*" He concludes: "*Louis Pouzin did not invent the Internet. But without the inventions of various contributors, including Louis Pouzin, there would be no Internet*". As American tech journalist Ben Tarnoff notes in The Guardian: "*the people who invented the Internet came from all over the world. They worked in places as diverse as the French computer network Cyclades, the National Physical Laboratory in England, the University of Hawaii, Xerox and Darpa.*"[42]

Louis Pouzin's version is very different: according to him, Vinton Cerf and Robert E. Kahn adopted the concept of the datagram (which Pouzin claims was his invention), with its notion of independent packets, after "*travelling around Europe in search of a solution to replace the Arpanet NCP, which was very limited*". So, the Americans "*visited the PTT, then came to see us and in the end, they chose the datagram.*" The researchers at Stanford and Darpa would have adopted the idea… while excluding the French computer scientist and his team. "*When discussing it together, we agreed that we would make changes to our system and that they would align themselves on ours to make it an international protocol. But Bob Kahn wanted to create a system in his own name so cunningly claimed that he couldn't do as we'd agreed because he was already too advanced in his TCP protocol project*", says Louis Pouzin. The computer scientist does not mince his words, and although he welcomes the work done by his American

---

[40] https://www.cs.princeton.edu/courses/archive/fall08/cos561/papers/cerf74.pdf

[41] "A Protocol for Packet Network Intercommunication", IEEE Transactions on Communications COM 22, 5 May, 1974. https://www.cs.princeton.edu/courses/archive/fall08/cos561/papers/cerf74.pdf

[42] "How the internet was invented", Ben Tarnoff, The Guardian, 15 July, 2016. https://www.theguardian.com/technology/2016/jul/15/how-the-internet-was-invented-1976-arpa-kahn-cerf

colleagues, he considers the Internet network as a *"copy of Cyclades"*, with *"datagrams, but also flow control requiring network intervention"*.

Valérie Schafer, as a self-respecting historian, keeps a neutral eye on the quarrels surrounding Cyclades, PTT, Arpanet and the Internet. But according to her, the Cigale network designed by Louis Pouzin and his team enabled French researchers to return to the center of international discussions: *"While initially, in meetings with Arpanet engineers, Cyclades members were mere 'guests', they quickly became actors in the debates and ideas"*. The network history specialist confirms that *"in the 1974 paper by Vinton Cerf and Robert Kahn, which defines the Internet's founding protocol (TCP/IP), we find ideas from the Cyclades network, in particular the datagrams, which were necessary not only for communication between computers, but also for communication between networks."*[43] The author of "La France en réseaux" notes that Cyclades *"was not the first"* packet-switched network, but that it was *"extremely pioneering"* in the choice of datagrams as compared to the virtual circuits adopted by PTT and even to a lesser extent by Arpanet. Finally, the historian adds, *"Louis Pouzin and his team demonstrated the effectiveness of this solution (without having developed a business model or a commercial network), and helped to disseminate this idea widely at European level (among the designers of the British NPL network, in particular) and internationally (during conferences, and through contacts with Arpanet). Thus the transfers of knowledge between French and Americans truly contributed to the fact that the datagram solution, more agile and more flexible, was retained for TCP/IP"*. But she further adds, *"the history of the Internet is not limited to the TCP/IP protocol"* (the Unix operating system, which is inexpensive and portable on several types of machines, having played a major role), and *"it is not a question of wondering if the Internet could have been French, but of studying the importance of context in the development of innovation. Making a packet-switched network was not only about having the right technical idea, it was also about evolving in the right environment, and that's what Cyclades lacked."*

In an article published in *Les Echos* in June 2008, journalist Charles de Laubier reports that on 29 March, 1973, a "decisive" visit took place in Rocquencourt, at the IRIA headquarters, by Vinton Cerf and Bob Kahn—who came to see "on site" the Cyclades team's work on the datagram: *"During a visit to the United States in 1972, Louis Pouzin spoke about his project to Vinton Cerf, a researcher at the University of California UCLA. Not believing his ears, the American went to IRIA on 29 March 1973, accompanied by Robert Kahn, who was in charge of developing a communication protocol for the Arpanet*

---

[43] ALOHAnet, developed in 1970 by the University of Hawaii to enable data communications between the islands, was based, for example, on radio transmissions.

network of the United States National Defense. *This meeting was decisive for Vinton Cerf: a first version of TCP/IP was developed in the fall of 1973*".[44]

For Pierre-Éric Mounier-Kuhn too, the role of Cyclades was decisive in the genesis of the Net. "*Technical formulas such as datagrams were developed in Cyclades and have become fundamental elements of the Internet, as we still know it today. Louis Pouzin and his team have also made a significant contribution to the creation and adoption of standards; as they were at the forefront, their engineers participated in the definition of standards at the international level, and this is a sign of technological strength, a sign that the French are recognized at the international level as competent people, who have been able to carry out technological developments that work at the operational level*", explains the IT historian.

Louis Pouzin says that once the PTT replaced his project with the X.25 in 1975, "*we completely stopped communicating with the Americans*", who reportedly refused his help. "*It was a big mistake, because it took them eight years to make the TCP/IP suite operational… They wanted to deviate from my protocol and that was a bad idea in fact! They introduced unnecessary complexities, including a loss of functionality, while the Cyclades system allowed the use of destination addresses that could be found in any system, regardless of the topology of the physical networks*", adds the retired computer scientist. For him, the protocol that created the Internet is imperfect: "*An IP address, in the United States, is always a number within the IP network. And if we want something else, we need a second protocol, for example HTTP. However, this system is burdensome when you want to do multihoming*"—i.e. to send data through multiple channels. According to the engineer, "*operators are forced to use an additional protocol to sort the amount of data sent… which is a huge waste.*" Despite Louis Pouzin's impression of having been "badly copied", the computer scientist has no regrets, disappointment or jealousy towards Bob Kahn and Vinton Cerf. "*Since we didn't file any patents, they don't owe us anything! In the end, the Americans saved the datagram! Because if they hadn't reintroduced it, we'd all be using the X25*", he says with a smile.

Web historian and curator of the Internet History Program at the Computer History Museum (CHM) in Mountain View, California, Marc Weber has been working on the history of the Internet and networks since 2007, date of the 30th anniversary of TCP/IP's beginnings, as it was first tested in 1977.[45] For over 10 years, the American historian interviewed the engineers behind this protocol (Vint Cerf and Bob Kahn), but also other network designers

---

[44] "La gouvernance du Net par les Etats-Unis n'est plus justifiée", Charles de Laubier—Les Echos, "Grand angle avec Louis Pouzin", June 21, 2008.
[45] Jon Postel, "NCP/TCP Transition Plan, RFC 801", ISI, Network Working Group, November 1981.

such as Alex Mckenzie and Louis Pouzin. If you visit the Museum of the History of Computer Science, you can find a detailed description of the Cyclades project in the gallery dedicated to the history of networks, which is next to the one dedicated to the World Wide Web. For Marc Weber, "*if he had had more budgets and political support, Cyclades could perfectly well have become the dominant network protocol. Cyclades' innovation is similar to the TCP/IP protocol… And clearly, Louis Pouzin is one of the engineers who invented a system of interconnected networks to connect people together. He did not do it alone, but his contribution is little known because his project did not succeed. Otherwise, he would have remained within the INWG, and he would have been one of the names quoted alongside Bob Kahn and Vint Cerf; he clearly influenced them in their work on TCP/IP, even if he did not work directly with them—it is an indirect contribution, within the INWG*". For Marc Weber, while Louis Pouzin is not "the only" Father of the Internet, he has in any case "*definitively influenced the architecture of TCP/IP, even if he lost the political battle.*"

According to Anne Pouzin, her father "*says it himself: The Internet has many 'fathers'. But he is undoubtedly one of them by having worked to spread the ideas at its origin, by talking about datagrams all over the world. He is, at heart, one of the 'spiritual' fathers of the Internet. He has worked hard for datagrams and OSI, and his rewards are well deserved*".[46]

With hindsight, Najah Naffah, who continues to see his former boss as "*someone very intelligent, very responsive and fast, who doesn't waste time on speculation and acts quickly; who supports his team, and coaches his men well*", and simply regrets his lack of "business acumen", which would have made Cyclades more "commercial". "*We weren't supposed to turn our ideas into a product, market them; there was no such culture in France at the time, we were thinking downstream, unlike the Americans, who acted first and then looked. And it's a pity that many products created at that time didn't have a market. Louis lacked the ability to transform research into a saleable product. He considered that his mission was to innovate, and that it was then up to others to do what was necessary to put his products on the market—in order to industrialize Cyclades*".

There remains the global impact of Cyclades in the history of IT and the Net. "*This project strongly influenced the decisions of ARPA, Vinton Cerf… But it was also very important in France from a business and social point of view, because it made it possible to train engineers, create a network culture, and allowed our industries, companies and researchers to acquire skills, to become network experts with IBM, HP, Sun…*", notes Michel Gien, for whom the IRIA project " trained a generation of engineers." "*Cyclades was an unforgettable adventure,*

---

[46] Interview with Anne Pouzin, 24 August, 2018.

a flagship project, which was not limited to theory: concepts were really put into practice, have been materialized in a computer network with a large geographical scope; and we demonstrated that French engineers were capable of reaching this level of development and maturation", adds Najah Naffah, nostalgic. "*At the time, it was a very beautiful, innovative project, which could be compared to the creation of the Concorde supersonic transport aircraft (operational in 1969), transposed in the IT field. We also had a considerable impact on the industry because we poached and borrowed many engineers and experts from service companies to contribute to the development of Cyclades, and who later returned to their companies. Thus, the know-how developed through Cyclades was highly beneficial to all the companies of the time*", he notes again. For the Franco-Lebanese engineer, "*if Cyclades did not exist, the Internet would have been created anyway. But we clearly contributed to the edifice in the form of protocols. As with any research which is inspired by other research, ideas are exchanged, some seize the opportunity for great successes, and others contribute with an idea…*" The dynamics of Cyclades also allowed, he concluded, "*Arpanet to demonstrate the international dimension of networks: we were able, through our existence, to validate the fact that when networks interconnect, it serves humanity, and can have an impact on a greater number of users because the more a network expands, the more users are affected and adopt it, and leverage it to create their own applications, which hadn't necessarily occurred to the creators of the original network*".

John Day, who was working at the time within the Arpanet project team, notes that "*the Cyclades project was also part of a singular period in the 20th century: the years 1960-1970*". This period was marked by unprecedented economic and industrial development in Western countries, as well as the construction of the European Economic Community (EEC), but also by wars (in particular that of Vietnam), decolonization and social conflicts (in France and the USA, in particular with the civil rights movement), computer researchers, who invented computer networks, but also microprocessors (1969), e-mail (1971) and the first personal computers (from the Programma 101 of the Italian company Olivetti designed in 1964 to the Apple II, launched in 1977 by Steve Jobs and Steve Wozniak), were real rock stars. "*The late 60s and early 70s were a very special time. Not just May'68 and the demonstrations in France, the US and elsewhere, but a very high degree of creativity that permeated everything. It was in the air everywhere! The Cyclades guys were part of that. Very much a part of it. And the degree to which that attracted us (and others) to them. They saw the problems as exciting as we did. I tell my students that in those days you could tell hardware people from software people by looking at them! We weren't just geeks, were also freaks (in the language of the day). For example, 4 of us left Urbana once to go to Philadelphia, as we got off the plane in Chicago, the flight attendant asked me if we were in a band! It was the same with the guys from Cyclades"*, he explains.

According to John Day, Cyclades' contributions to IT are numerous. *"The huge amount of technical innovation that CYCLADES was responsible for created a whole new paradigm of networking. A distributed computing model based on dynamic resource allocation, and recognition of the stochastic nature of traffic as opposed to the deterministic, asymmetric, static beads-on-a-string model of the ITU/CCITT/PTTs"*, he says. *"While layers were obvious to everyone, it was Cyclades where the current names of the layers (Physical, Data Link, Network, Transport, Application) were named and adopted. It is also clear that Cyclades had a deeper understanding of what layers were all about. Cyclades understood that layers were more general in networks than in operating systems. (There were no layer diagrams of the Arpanet Interface Message Processor subnet.) Cyclades was the first to show the whole network in terms of layers"*, he adds.

In the INRIA gazette, "Code Source", Louis Pouzin did not hesitate in 2007 to suggest that if Cyclades had lasted, *"we could have been the inventors of the Internet"*. He writes: *"One thing is certain, these were some of the most exhilarating years of my career, a truly euphoric time. (…) In 1975, the Cyclades network connected 25 computers in France, London and Rome as planned, on time and on budget. Despite this success, the project ceased to be funded to support another technology, the PTT Transpac network technology on which the Minitel was designed. I suppose Cyclades came too early in France. It was based on a packet switching technique—a concept called datagram—that had been developed in the late 1960s. However, this concept had not been implemented. We were the first to implement it. (…) Cyclades worked very well, and was used by the team of Jean Ichbiah, who died on January 26th, to develop the ADA language. Its concepts have mainly inspired the TCP/IP communication protocols of the Internet network. Datagrams were introduced in 1983 in the Arpanet network, then in its successor, the Internet. Which makes some people say we could have been the inventors of the Internet… Who knows?"*[47]

"It is difficult for a historian to predict what would have happened if Cyclades had not been stopped, we are not going to rewrite history; but it is as much the choice of datagram as this convergence of innovations around the world that created the Internet; and Louis Pouzin fully contributed with this idea of packets. If he hadn't talked to the Americans, different choices would certainly have been made…", Valérie Schafer cautiously argues. According to her, *"behind Louis Pouzin, the man, there is a whole era, a whole context, lots of traffic at different*

---

[47] "Code Source", "L'hebdomadaire des 40 ans de l'INRIA", "Louis Pouzin: le cœur de Cyclades", March 2017, p. 22.

scales; there was a profusion of innovations and contributions circulating. Louis Pouzin was influenced by a whole body of research on packet switching and by transnational traffic, in a French context that required him to make decisions and think about innovation in an open context." She adds that "*the Cyclades team was a pioneer, what it produced was cutting edge. But it was what Louis Pouzin designed, plus what the British NPL led by Donald Davies and Arpanet designed, that led to a major innovation that was structured over several years. So, it is a block within a much larger building.*" Finally, the historian defends the old Transpac network and its virtual circuits in her own way: "*It had a lot of short-comings, but it wasn't stopped until 2012, and one cannot say that the Minitel was a mistake. In the 1980s, this was not a mistake for France: for about ten years, the Minitel allowed France to have online services, electronic directories, messaging and much more; at a time when for the general public, there was no equivalent elsewhere. Because next to these millions of French people connected to online services, there were just a few communities, discussion groups like Usenet or The WELL (The Whole Earth' Lectronic Link) in the USA. It must therefore be recognized that in terms of the use of online services, Transpac and the Minitel were an important moment in the history of networks and digital technology.*"

For his part, Pierre-Éric Mounier-Kuhn willingly imagines an alternative history, one in which Cyclades does not replace the Internet, but contributes to it: "*the most realistic is a decision to keep the development of Cyclades as an experimental network for research, then a network linking more and more computing, physics and chemistry laboratories during the 1980s, and becoming RENATER (Réseau National de télécommunications pour la Technologie l'Enseignement et la Recherche—National Telecommunications Network for Technology, Education and Research) 10 years in advance.*" A network developed in 1993 by several research organizations, including CNRS, CEA, INRIA and INSERM, which "*will become a few years later one of the networks contributing to the Internet, one of the interconnected networks in the Internet*".

Finally, what was Cyclades' contribution to IT in France? "*There was a huge accumulation of experience, skills training which brought Americans and Europeans into the Cyclades team, and the two competing projects, Telecom and IRIA, proved that digital networks could be built, that it was not a futuristic dream for the year 2000, but that right then, in 1975 or 1978, we could implement digital networks that would then evolve and improve as IT and telecoms converged*", says Pierre-Éric Mounier-Kuhn. The project led by Louis Pouzin also served as a true talent incubator, according to Philippe Renard, the former engineer of the Délégation à l'informatique: "*Cyclades was a incubator for remarkable technical creators, who later disseminated their knowledge in other fields, developed technical careers—the late Hubert Zimmermann, for example, developed an OS competing with Unix, ChorusOS, and was hired by Sun Microsystems, which bought his product under license. Like any research project, Cyclades led to the development of expertise, which spread throughout the world, and I would say that Louis' ideas have spread more widely than Transpac's internationally; and in this sense, Cyclades was not a commercial success but was a technical success; and from the Delegation's point of view, there was enormous return on investment. Cyclades did not benefit France as a technical product, but greatly heightened the reputation of French engineers."*

6.4.1   Cyclades with Hindsight

With hindsight, Louis Pouzin wants to view the Cyclades project as a "beautiful adventure", without regretting its end. *"Any project must stop at some point. But it was an accumulation of knowledge, experience and personal relationships which was quite unique, after all. For me, it was an amazing, incredible opportunity the kind of project we were not accustomed to in France; not a huge project like the TGV, but an innovative project, considered as a project of hackers, with a small budget (we spent 20 million euros, but that's nothing at all, a trifle). But our efforts paid off much more than the TGV, due to the international recognition we received after that."* Far from being resentful, the retired IT specialist just regrets that his project ended *"in a rather stupid way on the European level"*, because, he explains, *"we had a big head start at the time, from which industrialists benefited, like the IT service companies SESA and STERIA, because of other company network projects that therefore did not require outsourcing to American companies. The SNCF network was designed by a French company, with datagrams (before moving to X.25 when this protocol became a standard). The same with the navy network."* While he still laughingly repeats that *"the American saved the datagram"*, he also regrets that the Americans did not keep "all the characteristics" of Cigale. *"We had defined that the recipient address was not a fixed point, hardware (an IP address), but a virtual point, located in the users' computers. Vinton Cerf and Bob Kahn's mistake was to consider addresses as physical points of network entry and exit"*, he explains.

For Louis Pouzin, the X.25 was never adapted to needs, even if technically it worked. So, he says, *"PTT saw packet switching as a closed system… They take packets, they transmit them, they deliver them, and they have done their job. But this is not what packet switching is all about: it is part of a much larger computer system. They should have had a much broader vision. With the datagram."* According to the computer scientist, *"the X25 protocol, preferred over the datagram, was much less reliable. Its use delayed the adoption of the Internet in Europe for over a decade.*" Louis also notes with a mischievous smile that today, "*the PTT must regret having supplanted us with the X25, because many people tell them that it was because of them that France lost control over the Internet, whereas it was very well placed*". However, fondly remembering the good old Minitel, he whispers: "*This machine was very useful to disseminate IT in everyday life, because it did not require any technical skills. In a way, it democratized computing.*" This assertion is therefore in line with Valérie Schafer's observations.

"*I agree with Louis: Transpac, the Minitel, was completely retrograde given the technology of the time. But we were researchers who depended on the Ministry of Research and the Ministry of Industry, and across the way we had the DGT, which was a state within state, a fortress, which explains why they won quite quickly... Even though technologically, the right way, the most efficient and intelligent one, was our approach, that of sharing dynamic resources. The proof is the Internet. And today, where is Transpac?*", laughs Jean-Louis Grangé.

Has Louis Pouzin, who seems so serene, had any bad spells? Does he have any regrets? Would he like more recognition? "*When Cyclades was stopped, I was a little lost, but I never wasted my time, I always stayed in motion, looking for other projects. No need to look back! Or to have regrets: I did what I had to do, that's all.*" According to him, much of his career has been based on unpredictable opportunities, not to say luck. The computer scientist has never laid out a career plan: "*It's a waste of time, it's better to take advantage of opportunities when they arise. The rest is based on initiatives: if I had decided to stay in the United States, at Bull, or in the Telco sector, I would surely have reached an important position. But I wouldn't have been happy.*" The inventor of the datagram is stubborn: "*You must always believe in what you are doing, listen to your instincts. At first, few people believed in the datagram, but I clung to it and finally, no one questions its usefulness anymore. In the Cyclades era, some people thought I was crazy, and I had many enemies. But as I often say, if you don't have any enemies, it's because you aren't doing anything interesting*", he laughs.

Today, Louis Pouzin is beginning to be recognized for his work, which contributed to the design of TCP/IP, and therefore the Internet. In September 1997, in Cannes, he was recognized as one of the "Fathers of the Internet" and as the "inventor and advocate of datagrams" at the ACM Sigcomm Award (organized by the "Data Communications" group of the ACM (Association for Computing Machinery), which he obtained alongside Jonathan B. Postel, former member of the Arpanet project.[48,49] In 2001, he was awarded an IEEE

---

[48] Petite biographie de Louis Pouzin et Jon Postel—SIGCOMM awards 1997, http://www.sigcomm.org/awards/sigcomm-awards/postel-and-pouzin-award-details

[49] http://conferences.sigcomm.org/sigcomm/1997/

(Institute of Electrical and Electronics Engineers) prize for "his contribution to the protocols that have enabled the development of networks such as the Internet". And on June 20, 2019, he was promoted to the rank of Officer of the Legion of Honor, the highest French order of merit for military and civil achievements.

Today, Louis Pouzin's work is also beginning to receive greater recognition from historians. *"As always in the world of research and ideas, it is those who develop them most broadly, on the surface, that are remembered. For many years, everyone thought that the datagram had been invented by the Americans, and I was never mentioned… But today, thanks to the work of Internet historians like Valérie Schafer, the truth has been restored"*, he says. *"You have to know that in life, there are a lot of people who have never received any recognition, even though they have done great things"*, Louis Pouzin puts things into perspective again. For example, who created the Web? *"Many people think that Tim Berners-Lee, a researcher at CERN, did it all by himself. But he had a colleague, Robert Cailliau, a Belgian engineer, who was totally forgotten whereas he did a lot of public relations work to convince CERN that Berners-Lee's concept was worth it, when no one believed in it."*

6.4.2   Disappointed Teammates/Luigi's Gang/A Great Adventure

All these distinctions and awards that are beginning to accumulate around Louis Pouzin cannot, however, hide the feeling of disappointment shared by many members of the Cyclades team… who consider themselves a little "forgotten" by their former boss. The Cyclamen remain very close, and regularly organize "Cyclades dinners"—an opportunity to remember the past and a friendly way to keep in touch, even 40 years later. *"After 1978, we continued to see each other. Unfortunately, two of us have since passed away, Hubert Zimmermann and Jean Le Bihan. But the rest of the team meets at least four times a year… We remain Luigi's gang"*, says Najah Naffah. Nostalgic, he still remembers the "extraordinary" atmosphere of the Cyclades project, which brought together "all very endearing" personalities. But meals between alumni have become increasingly difficult to organize in recent years—due to geographical distances or the age of the participants. *"Louis, he's a boss for whom I had a lot of admiration then (and still do today). We all did, the whole team. When we were young, we considered him our mentor. He had a great side, he was a funny, intelligent person with a rare sense of humor"*, says Jean-Louis Grangé, 73 years old today. *"As time went by, we all did other things, but Louis continued in this field and even today he is very active. He is referred to as the Father of the Internet. But in the team, some regret the fact that he almost never mentions his team. Listening to his lectures, it sounds as if he accomplished Cyclades all by himself, the Internet all by himself. Which is not very cool, and which makes some people, like Gérard Le Lann, take offense"*, he adds. *"Louis seems to attach no importance to the contribution his team was able to make, and to the fact that he is here today because of it, because he could never have done everything he did on his own. His awards are deserved! But what we can blame him for, even if he doesn't care about the rewards, is that he hasn't shared his glories with the people without whom nothing would have been possible… with his buddies."* To Louis Pouzin's credit, it should be recalled that the retired computer scientist has had several careers, the last one always being the most important. Always looking to the future, he has been involved in other battles where, apart from Jean-Louis Grangé, the others have never been involved but have all had satisfying careers. Louis has long taken a rather detached look at a possible biography of him. We had to be very insistent for him to accept the idea, he didn't see the point of such a book. What he wanted was for us to talk about the Cyclades project as a "collective story" and not just about him.

Anne Pouzin defends her father: *"At the end of Cyclades, in 1978, he found himself very isolated at the CNET, and his bitterness was greater than that of the other members of his team, who were younger and pursuing other projects. He felt like he had been isolated, sidelined. The fact that he does not quote his former colleagues often enough is not intentional; he just personally had a debt to himself. He wanted to prove that what he had done had value, and also that he was still in the game. His objective was not so much to be personally recognized but to have the French people realize that they had achieved great things. And since he was the one on the front line, and the others were busy working and had less time to deal with it, he explained what he himself had done, without any ulterior motives. He got into the habit of not talking about them, simply because they were on to other projects, and they never asked him to include them in his talks. This sort of thing doesn't occur to him so long as no one brings it up. He thought they were no longer interested… whereas Cyclades, Catenet and the networks remained his thing."*[50] *Louis Pouzin never planned to be in the spotlight, unlike his American colleagues. "Many people, especially academics, have gradually seen him as an important figure, symbolizing the presence of the French in the history of networks, to the point that an American researcher, a former member of the Arpanet project, John*

---

[50] Interview with Anne Pouzin, 24 August, 2018.

Day, chose his name[51] *for the website that showcases the work on the Internet of the Future, RINA".*

According to Anne, "*he didn't forget his friends on purpose, but he took them for granted... He was certainly always a little self-centered and crafty, and this defect has grown worse with age... but he just doesn't think about it. Especially because over the years, he has honed his speech, which is often the same at his conferences, and which has become a little fossilized.*" Louis still uses the colorful drawings made by Anne in his PowerPoint presentations. "*And finally, Vinton Cerf is much more self-centered than he is: he began his self-promotion much earlier, while my father started very late.*" Anne Pouzin concludes: "*None of this is intentional, and he was surprised that people were angry with him. Because it never occurred to him that putting himself forward may have resulted in putting other people in the shadows. He didn't even realize it.*"

Rémy Pouzin, 57, now electronics engineer at Alstom, notes that his father is "*very open, culturally and socially*", and also "*fundamentally non-violent*", thanks in particular to judo, which he has long practiced, at a high level. "*But he is also someone who easily ignores social conventions. Not that he's provocative, but he is unaware of them. He can very well show up on Christmas Day without gifts for anyone, for example... When you live in a world of scientific research, you live in a world apart, with fairly... offbeat habits. So, he does not pay much attention to social conventions.*"[52] He adds that the former director of Cyclades "*only cares about others in algorithmic terms: he communicates very well with others... but emotional management is not his thing. Recognition is a difficult thing for my father. For him, what is important is his technical work. The recognition of others is still important, and at a time when people are beginning to disappear, those who remain are even less tolerant that the work of those who are no longer there to claim it, like Hubert Zimmermann, has not been recognized. This kind of social and emotional abstraction is far too much for him.*" Rémy concludes: "*It's his main flaw, and it's not easy for him to manage; there are things that go wrong, unexpectedly, like sometimes the reaction of his colleagues, and in fact, he just doesn't understand what's going on... For him, as it's not important, he doesn't see why people complain when he says so*".

Beyond these defects and minor flaws, all those who have crossed Louis Pouzin's path agree that he is a great researcher and a good leader. "*At the international level, he is a very good communicator, in the noble sense: he knows how to convey ideas, motivate participants; I spoke with people who remember hearing him at international conferences, and who found that he eclipsed the other*

---

[51] The "Pouzin Society": http://pouzinsociety.org/
[52] Interview with Rémy Pouzin, 4 July, 2018.

speakers, because he not only had pedagogy, but also charisma and an ability to motivate around a project, to be convincing", says Valérie Schafer. *"Louis was a leader, the leader of a very solid team, a group of cowboys swept away by the adventure, which he led with conviction. There is an epic side to this whole adventure, as well as a great human, scientific and technological odyssey"*, she concludes.

For Michel Gien, 71, the Louis Pouzin whom he accompanied all over the world in the 1970s to develop Cigale, will always remain his "mentor". *"He supported. Like a master with his disciple, he instilled in me the pragmatic sense of doing things, not talking but doing, going all the way, and communicating differently: he was a storyteller before his time,"* says the co-founder and president of Twinlife. *"He instilled in us this way of behaving, being proactive, willing, confident, and telling everyone around us what we were learning. All this generated a dynamic in the development of technical computing in France; many former Cyclades alumni have created startups with an international scope. For me, Cyclades was at once a rigorous technical school, and a way of life. It was a pioneer era, and I was incredibly lucky to be a participant in this adventure."*

7

Louis Pouzin's "Retirements" (1993–Present)

7.1 The Hermit

In 1989, Louis joined Theseus, a management school for engineers and managers, in Sofia Antipolis. For 4 years, he taught computer and network technology. He lived in Antibes and discovered life on the Riviera: its climate, traffic jams and local activities.

He enjoyed organizing backcountry hikes using topographic maps, interacting with young and intelligent students and sharing his experience.

But, still as direct as ever and rather frank, he came into conflict with one of his colleagues, an American whom he considered a little narrow-minded. Moreover, the distance from Paris no longer allowed him to give courses and conferences, to be up-to-date on technological innovations, he missed it. As an accomplished traveler, he found it difficult to be satisfied with just going back and forth to Paris.

He decided to retire in 1993 at the age of 62.

In general, retirement is about doing everything you haven't had time to do during your working life. Back in Paris, single, separated from his wife, his children all grown up leading independent lives, Louis heeded his desires and resumed his computer development activities. He started to work on the specifications of PERL, a major programming language. The basic manual is 1189 pages long, he knows them all through and through. He was delighted to resume giving lectures and conferences, well paid at the time, alternating with solitary programming retreats. He says he was quite happy with his anti-spam program developed in PERL that he used for a very long time, an almost unknown utility in the early 1990s.

© Springer Nature Switzerland AG 2020
C. Lebrument, F. Soyez, *The Inventions of Louis Pouzin*,
https://doi.org/10.1007/978-3-030-34836-6_7

Louis' hermit side could have taken over, but the lectures and conferences became progressively less well paid and, more importantly, the topics were farther and farther from his true focus of interest, networks.

We are at the end of the 1990s, the Internet is now well established in France but poorly distributed, the monopoly of *France Télécom* and its prohibitive prices were not helping to democratize the tool. The term Web Giant or GAFA did not yet exist, Microsoft was predominant.

The Netscape Navigator browser was replacing the old Mosaic, there was even talk of watching videos online one day, but there were still only 56K modems. Uses still remained to be invented.

The French Internet community existed and was to be found at conferences and venues such as the Atelier Paribas,[1] created by Jean-Michel Billaut[2] in 1978. Its vocation is to reveal the full ICT potential of both companies and society, and now has branches in Europe, North America and Asia. The event has always been a favorite with the Internet community, showcasing French excellence in mathematics and science with typically Parisian Internet cultural knowledge.

7.2   The Autrans Internet Meetings

It was Bruno Oudet,[3] a professor at the University of Grenoble, who, on his return from Washington, launched the idea of meetings on Internet uses and took charge of organizing them. Louis had met him during one of his many trips to the United States where Bruno Oudet was Scientific Attaché at the French Embassy, where this *Papy Frog*[4] (his nickname) was already an Internet use professional. In this interview, saved from oblivion by the efforts of a group of volunteers who are doing their best to preserve key moments in the history of the Internet, he tells us: *"I have known the Internet for a long time since I had already made file transfers on Arpanet and on the French network Cyclades."*

Oudet was a tireless and imaginative worker who initiated, launched and maintained the FrogNet[5] network from March 1992. This network, the name being the acronym of French Research OrGanisation NETwork, distributed

---

[1] https://atelier.bnpparibas/en/about-us

[2] http://www.billaut.typepad.com/

[3] https://fr.wikipedia.org/wiki/Bruno_Oudet

[4] https://web.archive.org/web/20021205090232/http://www.france.com/mag/pfrog.html

[5] http://www.isoc.org/inet95/proceedings/PAPER/212/abst.html

daily information on France to more than 15,000 French-speaking expatriates and Americans. In 1994–1995, the information was relayed by Agence France-Presse and then by Radio France Internationale (RFI). It was the first successful electronic press in the world.

Having returned to France in 1995, Bruno Oudet wanted to create an entity along the lines of the Internet SOCiety World (ISOC World) to open France up to quality French content on the Internet and promote its use. A visionary, he had already planned a commercial web where economic development would have pride of place.

On February 26, 1996, Bruno Oudet, Christian Huitema, Bruno Mannoni and Thierry Piette-Coudol officially launched the French chapter of the Internet Society (ISOC France),[6] based in Grenoble, Bruno's home base.

At the same time, he launched the idea of an annual meeting based on the model of the ISOC World Congresses. A convincing man, he managed to bring others on board and the first meeting was held in January 1997 in Autrans. The Autrans Internet Meetings[7] were born: one week per year, in mid-January, in a remote place where politicians could not easily make an express round trip, came together a mixture of civil society, companies, geeks and developers… all dressed for the snow, and for life in a youth holiday center located 1 km from the village. They were all out of their element, only the wealthiest stayed in the Autrans hotels. For 10 years, this Internet week disrupted the peaceful life of the locals who were far more used to seeing sled dogs running around and skiers on the cross-country trails.

The meetings always went amazingly well, despite very haphazard organization with everything being done at the very last minute. Bruno was the one who held the community together, he excelled at putting his address book to good use.

One year the Quebecers presented their electronic schoolbag system, which was first introduced at the beginning of 2000, another year saw the first wi-fi tests using receiving antennas made from Ricoré® boxes (the *Ricoré Parties*, where participants emptied the village of all the 400g Ricoré containers they could find). There were also the 25 years of the Internet celebrated with Vinton Cerf, the magical discovery of a Virtual Reality helmet presented by Daniel Kaplan who had just created the FING[8] (Fondation Internet Nouvelle Génération), a presentation of virtual currencies by Jean-Yves Gresser, etc.

---

[6] https://fr.wikipedia.org/wiki/Internet_Society_France
[7] https://fr.wikipedia.org/wiki/Rencontres_internet_d%27Autrans
[8] http://fing.org/

It was a place where the abundance of ideas and surprising exchanges drew the entire Internet community, from 1997 to 2009 to a rudimentary holiday center for a week, lost in the middle of the snowfields of the Vercors. From 140 Internet users in its first year, some editions brought together more than 400 people. Autrans was an opportunity for people who had not seen each other in years to reconnect, to set up projects, it created a great dynamic for the French Internet.

The Autrans meetings were also opportunities for Louis to fight a number of misconceptions about the creation of the Internet and network management. He was increasingly active in the meetings to the point of neglecting his programming activities. During the plenary sessions he took pleasure in dismantling the arguments of the representatives of the American lobbies and forced people to face the issue of monopolies.

Thus, in the proceedings[9] of the second Autrans Meetings that ISOC France exceptionally published a few months after the reunion, we find on page 73 the transcript of Louis' speech in the plenary session: *"delighted that we are finally addressing a real problem: Microsod. It is a very serious threat. One could argue that this is not a monopoly but a racket. How is it possible that the American government has not yet put Bill Gates in prison?"* This speech stirred the audience up somewhat. The next day, January 10, 1998, he gave an interview which was hardly more moderate, *"I have nothing against Microsoft as such, except that it is a quasi-monopoly that destroys competition.../... It (Microsoft) finances products that it distributes free of charge to kill competition and then makes people pay, to finance a new generation of free products... That is dumping."*

For the 2000 session in Autrans, Bruno Oudet invited Christian Huitema, author of a famous book[10] on the beginnings of the Internet and who was once the champion of Open Internet. Having since been hired by Microsoft, he was copiously booed by the participants, to Bruno's great despair, he did not understand such ostracism. Interviewed by a French geek publication, *"Journal Du Net"*,[11] he defended his company, completely rubbing the French Autrans participants the wrong way.

The Autrans meetings held a special place in the life of the French Internet, something that the conferences organized in Hourtin in the Landes, which certainly drew crowds but only Parisians, politicians and advertisers in need of customers, never managed to do. People went to Hourtin to be seen and

---

[9] @ISOC France—"*Spécial Autrans 98*"—pp. 102–103.
[10] HUITEMA, Christian. "*Et Dieu créa l'Internet...*" Ed. *Eyrolles* 1996.
[11] http://www.journaldunet.com/solutions/itws/011126_it_huitema.shtml

deliver a speech written by aides but went to Autrans to discover the Internet and the full variety of network practices. Louis has never been to Hourtin.

Officially stopped in 2012 due to a lack of enthusiasm and a shortage of organizers, it was the end of an enchanting break in the very small emerging French Internet community. Friendships were born there, as well as hatreds and dislikes.

In the early 2000s, the Americans took control of critical resources such as Root and domain names. This was also a problem for language management because the Internet developed in the United States is in sub-American: the language developed for the network is in ASCII[12] (American Standard Code for Information Interchange) which does not allow any diacritics, not even those used in written English.

7.3   The WSIS

In 1978, at Tunisia's initiative, a request was submitted to the UN Secretariat for the organization of a World Summit on the Information Society.[13] The announcement in 1998 of a UN Summit to be held on the Internet in two sessions—the WSIS—left Internet users thrilled, and politicians confused. How to send Ministry representatives to a Summit to talk about a subject that was totally alien to them? In 1998 only civil society and a few companies mastered Internet access, the French ministries did not yet have email accounts, Internet users were still considered quite strange. As for politicians, the episode in which Jacques Chirac, inaugurating the François Mitterrand library, came upon a computer and discovered the mouse (which he called a "mole") left its mark in people's minds. At the same time, American Vice President Al Gore was at the heart of the digital revolution with a desktop computer, which he actually used. Politicians' ignorance was ridiculed by Internet users who couldn't decide whether to laugh or cry.

Moreover, it was impossible to imagine an Internet summit without Microsoft or ICANN (Internet Corporation for Assigned Names and Numbers), which are private companies. Faced with this difficulty, for the first time, the UN opened an official summit to non-governmental members. An ambassador and an official delegation were appointed for each of the countries represented at the UN, members of civil society could also

---

[12] http://www.tntbasic.com/learn/help/guides/asciicodesexplained.htm

[13] https://www.itu.int/net/wsis/index.html

participate, as well as companies, but all had to have credentials justifying real involvement in networks and the Internet.

Given all the positive things Louis Pouzin had to say about Microsoft, one can easily imagine his opinion on ICANN. In fact, it's his pet peeve. In addition to the very poor management of domain names, its main task and resource, ICANN still utterly refuses to do anything to make it possible to have Internet services in any language but English. Not all languages have been digitally translated and domain names are strictly in ASCII, much to the dismay of the Chinese, Russians, Thais, Europeans, Slavs, etc.

Unlike Cyclades, the development of the Internet by the Americans has not taken into account the diversity of users' languages. In 1961, the Department of Defense (DoD) developed an 8-bit standard data transmission code that was modified several times to produce ASCII, the first version of which was published in 1963. This coding does not even enable correct management of the American language and its diacritics, so other languages…

Louis took up arms on this new front: ICANN[14] and its abominable treatment of languages.

But Louis' passion for defending languages is not innocent because the American organization that has a monopoly on domain names is totally unable to meet this demand. The directors of the company are politicians: they are more administrators concerned with profits and side negotiations with the government than experienced technicians. Moreover, it is a very small, opaque structure: few employees, high salaries.

Thus, at the end of an evening in Autrans in 2001, in the foyer, the question of future participation in the WSIS brought together several of the usual participants. The idea of creating a structure to be accredited was launched. It would be a French not-for-profit (association loi 1901). The name and membership would be discussed at a future meeting.

After preliminary meetings of which Louis has forgotten the details, the launch meeting was held in Versailles in October 2002: the Eurolinc association was born (Official Gazette n°982 dated 7/12/2002). The Secretary General was Jean-François Morfin, the Secretary Jean-Pierre Henninot and Louis Pouzin was one of the members. Not surprisingly, one of the first goals of the association is:

* Defend and promote domain names using all characters and accents of European heritage languages;

---

[14] http://www.icann.org/

* Support technical and political analysis for a concerted vision of European ccTLD and .eu naming plans that meet the legitimate rights and expectations of users;

Between Louis' international notoriety and the creation of Eurolinc, accreditation to WSIS went smoothly.

Michel-Yves Peissik was appointed Special Ambassador for France to WSIS. The French Internet microcosm was small, and Michel-Yves Peissik was well known to the Internet community. He was an ENA alumnus, graduating in 1966 (the ENA is another French Grande École for training elites, "enarques" are integrated into the government as soon as they graduate). Michel-Yves Peissik had been Ambassador to many countries, including Yemen, Tunisia, Ukraine, Russia, he also worked in industry and was for several years Secretary General of IRIA (now INRIA)[15] and also permanent representative of France to ICAO (International Civil Aviation Organization),[16] a specialized agency of the UN, based in Montreal. He was also a regular at the Autrans Meetings for years.

Being familiar with UN bodies and having good knowledge of the research community, he was the right person for the job. His first reaction was to call Louis for advice, his second to create a list of delegates, discreetly adding Louis Pouzin and other Internet users he met in Autrans.

A UN summit is a high mass where everything is ordered according to immutable protocols. There are meetings, each with its own UN terminology. There are Intersessional Meetings, PrepCom1, PrepCom2 and even PrepCom3 and, after months of work, THE first Summit. All approved participants have the rank of United Nations observers, i.e. with diplomatic immunity within the meeting venues. Everything is interpreted into six languages, but only English is spoken. In short, a new world that Louis found very exciting and, most importantly, a place where the theme of Internet Governance quickly became the major concern, finally.

The PrepCom meetings from July 2002 to autumn 2003 were all held in Geneva, at the Palais des Nations or on the premises of the International Telecommunication Union (ITU). For more than a week, delegates from all countries met in meeting rooms or auditoriums for restless plenary sessions but, above all, in the cafeteria: this is where bilateral discussions took place and strategies were forged.

---

[15] https://www.inria.fr/en/
[16] www.icao.int/

An additional bonus for Louis was that the President of this first WSIS summit was the Malian Adama Samassekou,[17] a close friend of Michel-Yves Peissik's who was also a close friend of the then Director of the ITU, Hamadoun Touré.[18] All three had met in Moscow when they were posted and/or students there.

The French researcher Françis Muguet[19] was an activist who also played an important role in the choice of themes that were predefined for the Summit. Originally, there was no mention of access to knowledge or Internet Governance. These topics, which were considered to be of little interest, became the most discussed at PrepCom 1 (1–5 July 2002). During this summit, which was supposed to be one of fleshing out and debating, Francis literally harassed Adama Samassekou to obtain a room, a discussion, a text on his favorite subject: free access to scientific output. He even succeeded in reopening a debate that was considered closed. As Adama testified at Francis' funeral in 2009: "*Having had the great honor and privilege of chairing the preparatory process for the Geneva phase of WSIS, I can attest to the remarkable role played by Francis Muguet, on behalf of civil society, in the adoption of some key texts in the Geneva Declaration and Plan of Action, in particular the third fundamental principle "Access to information and knowledge", paragraph 28 on free access to scientific knowledge is his inspiration and almost his penship.*"

In 2003, Louis was made a Knight of the Legion of Honor by Claudie Haigneré, the first French woman in space, at the time Minister Delegate for Research and New Technologies in Jean-Pierre Raffarin's government. She is a woman of strong convictions familiar with the world of research, hence Louis' choice to receive this medal from her hands. A few months later, Claudie Haigneré gave the opening speech at the Intersessional Meeting at UNESCO Paris on 15 July 2003. Amidst the ICANN members and more than 750 delegates from around the world who had come to test the waters of this unprecedented UN summit, she said that "*thinking about new governance models has now become a strategic issue for companies and public organizations.*" And she adds: "*The Internet is global and cannot be monopolized by a single Nation-State*". This was a delicate topic, the role of ICANN and the United States' control over the Internet was not officially on the agenda, although was of course at the forefront of everyone's thoughts.

The Minister's speech was distributed in English at the break, which was a pleasure for everyone… except for the Chinese who were not very well

---

[17] https://www.itu.int/net/wsis/samassekou_bio.html
[18] http://www.who.int/topics/millennium_development_goals/accountability_commission/toure/en/
[19] https://fr.wikipedia.org/wiki/Francis_Muguet

equipped in translation in their delegation, they could only follow the simultaneous interpretation. The conference opening had taken them by surprise and they were not sure how to react, having no written reference to provide to their base in Beijing.

A representative of a French aeronautics company, SNECMA (now part of Safran Group), was working with a French-Chinese service provider who was pleased to translate the Minister's text in record time. After lunch, the text was printed in Chinese and distributed by future Eurolinc members to all Asian delegations. The Chinese did not forget this action and from then on systematically invited Louis Pouzin to their PrepCom meetings in Geneva. But Claudie Haigneré's attitude led delegations to believe that the French government would oppose the Americans, which was far from being the case, as these issues were not always well understood at the top. For the non-aligned countries, this Paris meeting is still remembered as "*the breath of freedom from Paris*". France still has this aura with WSIS delegates, without having officially or concretely done much to deserve it.

Louis Pouzin, on the other hand, was struggling to get the notion of Internet Governance recognized. With the support of Francis Muguet, he was able to invite participants to a tiny room, as it was believed that the subject would not attract more than a dozen people. Error: piled up at 25 at PrepCom 1, then in a room of 150 seats for PrepCom 2 (17–28 February 2003), then in an entire auditorium for PrepCom 3 (15–26 September 2003). All the non-aligned countries, with China, Brazil, Egypt, South Africa, Iran, India at the forefront, were determined to take up the issue of ICANN, much against the wishes of the United States. Thus, was created a group of *Like Minded Countries*, the cat was out of the bag.

For the PrepCom 3 weeklong meeting, the Chinese came back in full force, with a team of interpreters. They took the discussions on governance into their own hands alongside the Brazilians and South Africans and were very interested in Louis' technical discourse on the reality of an Internet root—nothing more than a database—and especially on the discovery that, contrary to widespread beliefs, there had been and still were other Internet roots[20] in the world besides ICANN's. During this lecture given at the last minute by Louis in an amphitheater that had been requisitioned at the last minute for the occasion, there was indeed a poor ICANN representative sent urgently to defend the dogma but he quickly understood that he was no match for Louis Pouzin's didactic and confident knowledge. The language issue is intimately linked to the question of Governance. Since the American monopoly wanted

---

[20] http://old.open-root.eu/documentation/realities-and-fairy-tales/a-brief-history-of-open-roots/

to avoid at all discussion on the internationalization of ICANN's root, the American representative took part in all the debates, but refused all requests and even went so far as to state that it was impossible to create domain names in any code other than ASCII. His ultimate argument was *"all they have to do is learn English, it's very simple"*.

There are many examples which show that ICANN's root is far from being unique but saying so came to nothing.

This summit was also an opportunity for Louis Pouzin to raise the issue of network monitoring by the NSA—*"if a country has the means to listen to everything and does not do so, it is idiotic"*. This was totally inaudible in 2003….

The official summit was held from 10 to 12 December 2003 and was a huge success[21] with no fewer than 11,000 participants from 175 countries. Louis was able to do what he loves: to chat, always just shy of provocation, going from one group to another to explain the DNS, Internet management, ICANN… Bilateral meetings between non-aligned countries to which he was systematically invited (thanks Ms. Haigneré!), those of the ITU Secretariat with Michel-Yves Peissik and Hamadoun Touré and finally, the friendship he forged with the president of the summit, Adama Samassekou, all allowed him to consider his participation a success. Always lucid, he never believed that the United States would give up the financial and especially political manna of the Internet to share with the rest of the world without a fight, but he feels that he was heard by representatives of countries that would have been inaccessible without this meeting.

The final declaration[22] states the main principles, even though the root of the Internet is still blocked on the Washington side and domain names are still being blocked in an ASCII language that is inaccessible to three-quarters of humanity.

But the non-aligned countries met and talked to each other. They also discovered that the Internet was not a technical problem but a political one. Mission accomplished.

The second Summit in 2005—normally the solutions Summit—had a different content, with the lobbies having been busy in the meantime. The group of *Like-Minded Countries* became the *Group of 77 + China* that a bad translation rendered as the "78 countries", the reference to the number 77 meaning in fact "a lot" in American slang.

In the French community, the first summit had the effect of strengthening ties forged in Autrans and clarifying positions. On the one hand, there were

---

[21] https://www.itu.int/net/wsis/geneva/index.html
[22] https://www.itu.int/net/wsis/documents/doc_multi.asp?lang=en&id=1161|0

the participants of the dogma of the single root, indivisible and very well managed by our American friends, and on the other hand, those who returned from Geneva with the conviction that the technical arguments were over, and the struggle was now political. For example, AFNIC, the French organization that manages TLDs, including the .fr, issued a press release[23] stating that "*the Internet user wants to work in security, transparency, trust and needs a universal naming service managed in the public interest.*"

---

[23] https://www.afnic.fr/fr/l-afnic-en-bref/actualites/actualites-generales/2579/show/position-de-l-afnic-sur-la-racine-internet-unique-faisant-autorite.html

8

Internet Governance (2005–2012)

8.1 A Fragmented French Community

But the *chiaroscuro* of existence leaves room for all shades of opinions, from ISOC France, which remains true to its parent company (and therefore to ICANN), to the members of Eurolinc, which has become a recognized entity in the French landscape as has Louis Pouzin, a troublemaker who delivers provocative messages.

Louis never tires of bashing ICANN and its affiliates. The Geneva experience confirmed his position that it is untenable to have a monolingual Internet, with no resource sharing and full cultural lockdown. The moving speeches on the sharing of resources and the promotion of ICT (Information and Communication Technologies) for development do not hold water when one observes the negotiation sessions between the American ambassador and the other countries. The United States hasn't given in on anything? "*That's perfect, says Louis, impassive, it can only serve to show the world that this imposed model is not viable*".

8.2 The Defense of Natural Languages

After this first phase of the WSIS Summit, Louis returned to battling on one of his favorite governance topics: the use of languages, multilingual domain names, the monopoly of root management, subjects which were debated and amplified within the Eurolinc association. The contacts made through the

© Springer Nature Switzerland AG 2020
C. Lebrument, F. Soyez, *The Inventions of Louis Pouzin*,
https://doi.org/10.1007/978-3-030-34836-6_8

Geneva process were leveraged and the launch of the second phase (Tunis) provided opportunities to raise these issues with the delegates.

After being very present in Geneva, the Chinese became more discreet: they had other priorities than a UN high mass about which they harbored no illusions. In fact, since 2005 they had been implementing the technical precepts discovered at the WSIS in Geneva. A country receptive by nature to central government orders, the Chinese simply created their own root, in Mandarin. By the end of 2005, they were independent of the American root managed by ICANN, although it was not until 2007 that the media began to notice this, exemplified by Gordon Cook's article[1] about an IPv9 network, making it clear that it was a new root and not a protocol. Five years later, the Chinese network was broadcast throughout the country, under the direct authority of the Ministry of the Interior and Information (MII). It is broadband and closely monitors Internet users, but the development of the country and e-commerce are a reality and more than 12 years after its creation, millions of Chinese people are logged into this huge network, with limited interactions with the ICANN system. The Chinese reality is being imposed on the world through the giant e-commerce companies that compete with the American Gang of Four. There are currently reportedly three Chinese Internet roots, it is easy to find the MII Root and its DNSs, for the others, please contact the Party.

At the beginning of this century, there was much talk of Internet Governance, linguistic and cultural diversity, monopolies but rarely security. However, the Internet was already a sieve and groups of hackers had been operating with impunity on the web since its inception. The official annual meetings of the DEF CON©[2] began in 1992, the meetings called *2600*[3] in the 1980s. Now that they have become very ethical, it is important to remember that the first meetings of the *2600* were held in cafés in San Francisco, Montreal or New York. Attending them was either a rare privilege or a stroke of luck.

The years 1970–1980 were marked in France by the astronomical telephone costs and the resourcefulness people deployed to communicate at a lower cost. Louis explains: "*I had discovered that it was possible to make free calls using Parisian public telephone tokens. All you had to do was put the token in, dial the number and hang up right away… and the call was established, free of charge*". Tinkering, always tinkering. An enthusiastic user of the Minitel, Louis

---

[1] http://www.circleid.com/posts/813112_china_internet_root_ipv9/
[2] https://defcon.org/index.html
[3] https://www.2600.com/

connected to the network by modem, like all Internet users in the 1980s, but still has his installation in working order. The obligation to connect in the evening to benefit from France Telecom's off-peak rates is a joy for this night owl who loves to write his articles during sleepless nights.

At the international level, Louis Pouzin is known and recognized, articles, interviews and invitations fill his agenda. But in France, he is still the black sheep. Even though he has been awarded the *Chevalier de la Légion d'Honneur* and has received numerous awards, there is still a whiff of sulphur about him in the eyes of the French community, which does not understand his opposition to ICANN and the emerging GAFAs. The NSA and its oversized ears? An article published in the New York Times revealed its existence as early as 2008. Louis Pouzin never misses an opportunity to recall the various Internet registration programs at international conferences where delegates listens with interest and discover with surprise the existence of Open Roots (domain name management systems outside the US monopoly).

On the security side, Louis has always maintained that the Internet is built on sand, and that it is a test version that was not intended to become the support for global development. But in France, until the Snowden case[4] in June 2013, talk about US surveillance was considered paranoia. He was unable to make himself heard on this subject for a long time, and was either not believed or, worse, attacked.

Between 2003 and the new summit in 2005, the time frame was short, but progress was made. The three PrepComs were held in Hammamet (June 2004) and Geneva (February and September 2005). Lobbies had had time to organize and challenges to ICANN were less vigorous because delegations had understood that it would be to no avail, but bilateral discussions were still just as active.

For this summit, there was a new President, and France sent a new ambassador, but this time Louis Pouzin had pride of place within the French delegation[5] to Tunis. This was the summit of solutions with a final resolution.

The difference between the two summits also lies in the locations, from Geneva to Tunis, which became a closed city for the occasion. Opponents and local activists were gagged, the country welcomed the thousands of participants in the false atmosphere of a county fair. The official delegations, already numerous at the first Geneva Summit, put on a show: between the Vatican and its geek prelates and Bhutan in traditional clothing, prostrating themselves before the representatives of their monarchy and sweeping the ground

---

[4] https://www.theguardian.com/world/2013/jun/09/edward-snowden-nsa-whistleblower-surveillance
[5] https://www.itu.int/net/wsis/docs2/tunis/final-list-participants.pdf

before their king, people hurrying to attend official meetings… but the real work was done in small overheated rooms where people busily unraveled and rewrote the text of the declaration called the "Tunis Agenda". Once again, the Americans were blocking any in-depth discussion, they came in force and were to be found in every session. Everything was subject to negotiation, an entire night was spent on punctuation, a day on reducing the number of so-called [brackets], to ensure there would be a declaration to sign during the final ceremony.

Meanwhile, documents started circulating on parallel events being held in town. "Delegates" would sometimes disappear "into the city" for meetings away from surveillance (Tunisian, NSA and others).

This was the case for Louis Pouzin. In Geneva he had spoken with the Koreans (among others) and in particular with Pan Jeong Lee (alias P.J.). This clever Korean entrepreneur is the founder of Netpia[6] and is known in Korea for inventing a keyword system that replaces Internet addresses and thus allows smooth navigation in Korean, a language very different from ASCII. Netpia held its first demonstrations in February 1999 in Korea, China and Japan.

P.J. says that the then Korean president was elected by putting his name as a keyword on his posters.

Ten years later ICANN copied his system by adapting it more or less well to ASCII and by working with the UNICODE consortium to launch IDNs (Internationalized Domain Names), i.e. domain names in non-ASCII characters that all start with the prefix xn-.[7]

To prepare for the Tunis WSIS, P.J. created the NLIC (Native Language Internet Consortium) in November 2005 to promote multilingualism on the Internet. Most of the members of this group are countries whose languages do not use Latin script (Greece, Turkey, Maghreb, Korea). Initiated after the Geneva discussions, the NLIC formed its Bureau during the WSIS in Tunis, and Louis Pouzin was appointed President. He remained so for several years and is still active in P.J. Lee's initiatives.

---

[6] http://en.netpia.com/

[7] https://tools.ietf.org/html/rfc5890

8.3   The Post-WSIS World

Not unexpectedly, the final WSIS was a flop. The Tunis Agenda contained nothing revolutionary and, above all, the United States made no concessions. Although Governance was a central theme, the only response was to create an annual Forum on the subject. The Internet Governance Forum (IGF) was tasked with continuing discussions and reporting on country achievements. A decision-making body, the MAG (Multistakeholder Advisory Group), was created and chaired by the United Nations Secretariat, in other words more fluff, especially since the question of funding was never settled. Without resources, under pressure from lobbies, the IGF is now in ICANN's hands with a system of revolving doors between the two structures.

But the summit was a success in that it enabled the creation of a follow-up forum for initiatives, the WSIS Forum.

Remaining within the framework of ITU, and therefore the United Nations, its objectives are: *"In accordance with the Tunis Agenda for the Information Society, the WSIS international implementation mechanism should take into account the main themes and broad orientations set out in the Geneva Plan of Action. ITU, UNESCO and UNDP have a leading role in the implementation of the Action Plan"*.

The main work streams of this action plan are divided into 11 categories[8] and annual meetings are still held in Geneva. Always an occasion for meeting people from around the world and discovering new achievements, the event is a permanent fixture on Louis' agenda. He makes the trip to Geneva every year, at his own expense.

Because after the WSIS, Louis took up his pilgrim's staff again and went back to traveling the world, after a professional career spent on planes. But in retirement, without a sponsor (but with enemies), accepting conferences and participating in international meetings became more complicated.

Over the years, a travel agent-like organization has grown up around Louis: finding the best flights and accommodation at the lowest prices. There was a beach diving club in Egypt for the 2009 IGF, a hut in a seedy motel in Zambia for an AfriNic meeting where the toilets at the bottom of the garden overlooked the jungle resounded with roars that made it difficult to sleep, the superb hotel in Hyderabad, India, in a street which was unfortunately under construction and therefore inaccessible… Sometimes group travel has been used, gathering together relatives, Eurolinc and other association members, various acquaintances, etc.

---

[8] http://groups.itu.int/stocktaking/About/WSISActionLines.aspx

As for the IGF, Louis systematically attends the meetings, having missed only one between 2006 and 2018: it was held on a beach on the Brazilian coast and was both too complicated to access and too expensive.

Skirmishes between Louis/Eurolinc and ICANN continue, given that the members of the IGF MAG are sponsored by the American organization, due to a lack of budget from the UN.

Despite attractive workshop proposals on the part of Eurolinc, only two have been accepted in 12 years: one for the first IGF, in Athens in 2006, where Eurolinc brought along the great Indian chief of the Cree tribe, Matthew Coon Come to present their cuneiform syllabic alphabet,[9] and the second for the IGF in Istanbul in 2014 because it was necessary to find a spot so that a professional wannabe could travel for free. A workshop was once granted on Day 0 (not on the official program, no publicity, but a room) at the Bali session in 2013 where Louis was able to present the work carried out by "La Boîte à Innovations"[10] in Africa with its exemplary digital literacy system. Francophone Africans are particularly penalized at these UN meetings because only the plenary sessions, which are generally of no interest, are interpreted. Thus, Louis' bilingualism and knowledge of the subjects has helped the African community on several occasions.

When the first IGF was held in Athens in 2006, there was an edifying experience: a workshop proposed by the Chinese where they demonstrated multilingual email. It took place in a room so crowded that Vinton Cerf was practically sitting on the floor in the first row. In real time, the presenters sent an email with an address entirely in Chinese which was received a few minutes later on an IGF computer connected to a giant screen (no cheating possible, it was all live). Vint jumped up and touched the screen to be sure he was not dreaming: the Chinese in Singapore had found the solution for a multilingual Internet and it was not through ICANN.

For the Istanbul workshop in 2014, the session managed by Eurolinc was the last of a long list, located at the end of an exceedingly long corridor. By the time the UN delegate had finally activated the broadcast button to enable remote participation, time was up, the session was over. The session was recorded and officially validated, but no interaction with Internet users had been possible. Examples of systematic sabotage abound. Since then, no other workshop proposals have been accepted, even though Louis, with French and Belgian colleagues, applies each year, with renewed themes all based on multilingualism and the technological advances essential for the Internet.

---

[9] http://www.omniglot.com/writing/cree.htm
[10] https://bai.alphaomedia.org/

Louis and Eurolinc have always been a thorn in the side of those who are opposed to transparent Internet Governance and Multilingualism. Louis' position has never wavered, he is unconcerned with critics. When he believes in an idea, he sees it through no matter what. As he likes to say, this is his third retirement, they can bring it on, he's been around the block a few times and nothing reaches him, well, almost nothing.

8.4   Open Roots

Let us now return to the legend of ICANN's single root. A root is what manages the domain name system that translates the IP addresses of machines in a network into a name that is understandable to humans. What is called Top Level Domain or TLD is the first level, the one that is searched when an Internet user enters a query. The official root server is managed by ICANN but there are other root servers managed by other entities, with their own servers and the ability to create their own TLDs. During a lawsuit brought by *Name Space*[11] against ICANN, it was discovered that in the portfolio of several hundred domain names managed by the latter, one hundred and eighteen had misappropriated by the American organization for its own benefit: .cafe, .opera, .time, etc.

However, a domain name has no intrinsic value. The root is only a database generating simple files in list form (an Excel file). Once the TLD has been put in a root—which requires technical expertise and has high added value—adding a domain name requires a modest amount of work at first, but none thereafter. ICANN's model based on rentals which need to be renewed on a regular basis is racketeering, and it is scandalous that this private company is officially allowed to hold the monopoly.

There are nonetheless providers managing what have long been called "alternative roots"[12] but which Louis prefers to call "open roots", contrary to those of ICANN, which are closed and controlled by the US government. The attacks and contradictions of lobbies and official institutions which venerate all things American hold no sway with him.

At the end of WSIS in 2005, Louis researched and met with all small groups or pseudo-companies boasting they could offer TLDs on demand. From 2008 he also turned to politicians with a concrete example: the French domain name of a masonry company located in Angers, which had the URL www.

---

[11] http://old.open-root.eu/about-open-root/news/a-rough-take-off

[12] https://icannwiki.org/Alternative_Roots

maconneriedangers.com—literally "my mistakes, danger"—advertised on the side of a van. Louis found this hilarious and it is indeed a great way to illustrate the problem with not being able to use diacritics, essential for communicating in French but not supported by ASCII.

After reaching out to quite a few people and making several trips, Louis contacted a group of German activists in 2008 who had recently joined the Bundestag as the Pirate Party: all their logistics had been based on an open root and a DNS in .pirates. Solid technicians, honest, discreet and efficient, they were familiar with the mysteries of the DNS, knowledge shared by few. In general, system administrators tend to rely on commercially available and recognized hardware where everything is already configured... by Microsoft. Using hardware with Open Source Software and installing your own DNS management system is not within everyone's reach, managing a root requires rare skills. These Germans had already been taught by colleagues across the Atlantic and their network covered Greater Europe and the American continent. Working with Louis is quite exciting, he is always open to new ideas, thinks fast and with an unstoppable logic he will systematically find the flaws in your thinking, in your system. The Cesidian Root team was therefore pleased to welcome this new member, in his seventies at the time but incredibly dynamic. Louis now works with a network managed from Mexico, with servers on all continents.

On a personal level, however, Louis manages his digital life in a highly unusual manner. He has no cell phone (instead he has several, some of them obsolete), no direct involvement in social networks (he relies on his entourage for that) and his computer workstations are the most obsolete possible. To be admitted into Louis Pouzin's life, the conditions for a laptop are weight (less than a kilo), size (it must fit in his handbag) and processor (W8 if necessary). Eternally absent-minded, deaf (he removes his hearing aids when he wants to think), he regularly loses his machines during trips, often too tiring for him. In Istanbul it was the blue computer that remained on the floor of the navy-blue restrooms at a restaurant. In Romania it was the grey one that remained on the train table of the same color... and, being the connection junkie, he is, the number of times his machines have crashed, sometimes in the middle of presentations, are no longer to be counted. As far as his data are concerned however he is inflexible and has developed a personal system that ensures that he never loses his information, nor leaves it lying around.

9

Recognition (2012–2015)

9.1   Louis Pouzin, Pariah and Outcast

Louis has received numerous awards but the one from April 2012 stands out: it was granted by ISOC World and recognizes Louis' lifetime achievement and significant contributions to the development and advancement of the Internet, notably for his role in the invention of TCP/IP, despite all the turbulence in 2008–2009. Louis is thus honored as one of the pioneers of the Internet and registered at the Hall of Fame in Geneva.

Despite this recognition, in February 2013, one of the worst French trolls, whose name we will keep silent for the time being, attacked Louis yet again, implying that he had never invented anything, that he was a spoiled brat and that in fact his reputation was groundless. Despite being accustomed to criticism, these attacks were harsh and left a bitter taste: after having fought so hard to advance the cause of the Internet, the French were still trying to kill it symbolically. Especially since the organization from which the attacks stemmed protected the troll and in fact supported him. But Louis remained impassive and never responded, as is his wont. That being said, his answers to certain questions can be scathing. For example in response to an often asked question on ICANN's role in the Internet, Louis, very professoral, explained that it was only a racket and that the "*icannards*" were a mafia…

Despite being a scientific researcher, Louis Pouzin is above all a handyman who loves to create things and follow through on his achievements. In June 2012, Savoir-Faire SAS was created; in November of the same year, the Open-Root website was launched. Its business model contrasts with that of ICANN: TLDs are sold outright at a very reasonable cost, implementation of domain

© Springer Nature Switzerland AG 2020
C. Lebrument, F. Soyez, *The Inventions of Louis Pouzin*,
https://doi.org/10.1007/978-3-030-34836-6_9

names is free, and purchasers have global access to the name servers of the Open-Root network… to the amazement of many. An 82-year-old entrepreneur, he spares no effort to make his offer known, always sufficiently mysterious to keep his interlocutors guessing. His ability to move forward is inversely proportional to his management of the past: who has ever heard him brag about inventing the *Shell* language? About having succeeded in setting up a Pouzin Team that produced a national weather management software, *Meteos*, which was used for 15 years? About having spoken at hundreds of international conferences that have taken him around the world several times.

9.2   The QEPrize

On March 18, 2013, 3 weeks after the hateful troll attack, Louis learned that he would receive the **Q**ueen **E**lizabeth **P**rize for **E**ngineering (QEPrize) from the Queen in June. In fact, Louis first of all received some calls on his home line which mentioned Buckingham Palace. Not being fully focused and not wearing his hearing aids he concluded it was spam… and hung up. The Queen's Secretariat had to call him in person to give him the news.

For the retired engineer, the most heartwarming recognition of his work has come from the United Kingdom, namely the QEPrize which he was awarded alongside Bob Kahn and Vinton Cerf, as well as Tim Berners-Lee and Marc Andreessen, in 2013, from the hands of the Queen herself.[1] An award for their "*major contributions to the creation of the Internet and the World Wide Web*". Since then he has met the queen three times (she likes this "Frenchie" who is the same height as her and speaks such good English) but the secretariat reminds him of this episode every time.

"*I'm pretty immune to rewards, but it's still good to get them!*" laughs the network pioneer. He explains that "*it is useful to be recognized, because it easily opens doors. But as far as I'm concerned personally, prizes are trinkets which have no impact on my mentality or way of life.*"

Today hailed as one of the founding fathers of the Internet, and as a researcher who, while not inventing the network of networks, still contributed greatly to it, Louis Pouzin was especially recognized for his work outside his own country, rather paradoxically, especially in England. "*No one is a prophet in his own country, says the proverb*", laughs Louis Pouzin. "*But you have to keep in mind that when we carried out Cyclades, we were known all over the world – by the Russians, English, Americans…*", he says.

---

[1] http://qeprize.org/winners-2013/louis-pouzin/

For the awards ceremony in June 2013, Louis came bearing gifts for the Queen: excellent wines, French artwork (thank you Michèle!) and an open root TLD, the. QEPRIZE. Even though very up to date on engineering, it is doubtful that Her Majesty understood the meaning of this gift, which was nevertheless used by her teams as a stealthy global extranet for their exchanges.

The QEPrize was a turning point in Louis Pouzin's life. His positions and convictions can be criticized, but at least his actions are recognized. This award gave him a visibility that he did not formerly have (and in fact did not seek to have). In interviews with journalists, in cafés or in friends' apartments, his own being impenetrable,[2] he does manage his career to a certain extent, but the prize finally enabled him to explain the importance of naming in the Internet and open roots. He lives firmly in the present and the future, never expressing bitterness about the past. His confounding frankness, his precise vocabulary and his mastery of a wide variety of subjects are a major factor in the fascination he exerts on those around him. He is a brilliant speaker who is full of anecdotes, with a very dry British humor that brings great enjoyment to those who interview him, often going well beyond the appointed times.

The year 2013 was entirely devoted to managing this sudden notoriety which took him completely by surprise. It was also the year of the Snowden affair… and Louis could easily remind people that he had been warning them about the activities of the NSA and the FBI for a long time. In 2008 he talked to whomever would listen about Mark Klein, an ATT engineer who worked at one of their centers in California who had realized that all ATT international communications were being redirected to the NSA, totally illegally. As he wrote in the École Polytechnique journal[3]: "Let us recall here the Edward Snowden case and, previously, the little-known story of Mark Klein, an engineer at ATT, who discovered in 2002 that a major communication artery was being copied to the NSA. Having left ATT, he tried for months to convince newspapers to reveal this illegality. The New York Times finally agreed to publish this information after agreeing with the FBI to delay publication by one year in 2005. No media reaction followed."

The Electronic Frontier Foundation (EFF) sued the U.S. administration to obtain reports that had been published internally on this trafficking with the NSA, in vain to the best of our knowledge.

---

[2] Louis keeps EVERYTHING, especially conference hand outs and proceedings, sometimes stacked up in the middle of the room for months before someone takes the initiative to "classify" them. He has numerous devices that museums would love to get their hands on.

[3] https://www.lajauneetlarouge.com/article/internet-le-liberalisme-au-service-de-limperialisme (only in French)

9.3   Cybersecurity

After having fought for languages, against the single root, for shared Governance, cybersecurity became Louis' pet interest in 2013. In this respect, Louis Pouzin received strong support from those who are in daily contact with the misdeeds of hackers and the naivety of Internet users: the French cybergendarmes. These professionals understood very early on that nothing would happen in digital development without network security and that France's sovereignty was at stake.

The International Cybersecurity Forum (FIC—Forum International de la Cybersécurité) High Mass is organized by cybergendarmes under the leadership of General Marc Watin-Augouard and aims to "*open up the cybersecurity debate by bringing together digital transformation players, risk management specialists […] to promote innovation in the service of digital trust*".

Their great success has put France back among the European leaders in this area. The FIC celebrated its tenth anniversary in 2018 and, given the quality of the edition,[4] it is now an essential event that finally brings together not only major French companies and political leaders but also European and international stakeholders.

It must be said that there were several significant attacks around the world in 2018 and that, even though those who are targeted did their best to hush it up, French companies were no exception. Andy Greenberg, in his book *SandWorm*, reprinted in an article in *Wired*[5] entitled "*The Untold Story of NotPetya, the Most Devastating Cyberattack in History*", recounts the disaster caused by *NotPetya* and talks about a \$384 million loss for *Saint Gobain*. According to *Deloitte*, which surveyed nearly four hundred companies of all sizes among its clients in France during the second half of 2017, 63% of IT security incidents were caused by an active employee.

Founder and organizer of the FIC, General Watin-Augouard is convinced that "*in the next fifteen years, a massive transfer of criminal phenomena from the real world to the digital space will take place. If the international community fails to agree on common standards, if cybersecurity policy does not rise to the challenge, if citizens, companies and States do not become aware of it, the future will be bright for the 'new barbarians'*". Similarly, Guillaume Poupard, head of the French National Agency for Information Systems Security (ANSSI), is working hard to raise awareness of the importance of cybersecurity. He knows what he is talking about, his mission is to protect from cyber-attacks the most

---

[4] https://www.forum-fic.com/en/home/discover/back-on-2018-edition/2018-content.htm

[5] https://www.wired.com/story/notpetya-cyberattack-ukraine-russia-code-crashed-the-world/

sensitive State structures and Operators of Vital Importance (OIV—Organismes d'Importance Vitale), companies operating in essential sectors of activity (energy, health, banking, transport, etc.).

Louis Pouzin's many talks on cybersecurity and especially on the Internet root managed by Washington could only be music to these professionals' ears. During the 2017 edition, at the last minute he replaced a minister who had not yet shown up to give the inaugural speech of the FIC and spoke frankly about the fragility of the Internet and the reality of the fragile state of digital sovereignty in Europe. He ended his speech with a call for Europeans to wake up and regain control of their data. Disappearing behind a desk too high for him, with a voice ragged with fatigue due to an insane agenda for a person over 85 years old, he nonetheless spoke with great conviction. It was a huge success.

There is now a "Louis Pouzin" building on the cybergendarmes' premises in the northern suburbs of Rennes (Brittany), and, in Cergy-Pontoise, near Paris, a room bears his name at the judicial center of the national gendarmerie (lPJGN).

9.4   Louis Pouzin, Recognized… Abroad

Another prize, another universe: in August 2015 Louis received an email informing him that he was the winner of the *2015 Lovie Awards*[6] with a Great Prize, Special Achievement category (a detail he hadn't noticed when he received the document at home). Another email that was classified in the "to be read" or "reply" section, even worse in the Pouzin message reception classification. After verification, yes, the event exists, the nominees are all elected by an international council of experts and it is even a very popular event in London life. Yes, once again, Louis is distinguished by the English.

The *Lovie Awards* ceremony rewards the best in the European Internet each year, and here is what the British grantor said when he presented his award to Louis: "*By the sobriety of his invention and the simplicity of his resolution of the transfer of data packets, Louis Pouzin has laid the most important foundation stone in the creation of the Internet.*"

The ceremony was scheduled for the last weekend of October 2015 which was not a good time as the second invitation from Buckingham Palace was for just a few days later, on Friday, November 13, a trip that promised to be exhausting as Her Majesty would not be taking care of logistics this time so he

---

[6] https://www.lovieawards.eu/

had to make the round trip during the day (the return in the evening was somewhat disrupted by the series of attacks that hit Paris that day). For the *Lovie Awards*, making contacts, making appointments for interviews, receiving tickets, charming people on the phone, everything was done to encourage Louis to come and receive the distinction. What he didn't know was that he was the award winner for the Cyclades project and the invention of the datagram and that he would be the main feature of the ceremony, hence the subtitle of the invitation, Special Achievement.

It was a significant moment both for the quality of the organization and for the symbolism of the award. The organizers had taken things to a new level with the production of a video clip[7] explaining the ingenuity of the datagram, produced by an American company in New York, a special Louis Pouzin postcard and a London reception in a trendy location. During the ceremony Louis made his speech, as usual, then received a standing ovation of several minutes by a packed room where the average age did not exceed 30. This had not happened to him for a long time, as far as he could remember the last time had been in Toronto at the ICCC meeting in 1976 during his pro-datagram and anti-telco presentation that angered his then IRIA director, André Danzin.

Being officially distinguished by international experts for the datagram and being the subject of a selfies race throughout the evening by young fans hysterically excited at the thought of meeting him were special experiences.

At the international level it was something else: Louis was not only recognized but sometimes even invited to be the official host.

This was the case with Her Majesty in 2013 for the granting of the QEPrize from Queen Elizabeth II on June 25, 2013 at Buckingham Palace. He saw Her Majesty again in 2014 during her visit to Paris, within the walls of the British Embassy, where he was very well placed, among the British guests! And totally ignored by the entire French government sitting across from him. Similarly, in 2015, at the second QEPrize ceremony, where the guests presented themselves in single file upon being announced for a brief handshake and a few gracious words. This brief respectful bow seems to have been too brief for the Queen who asked to spend more time with "this little Frenchman who speaks English so well". Although a photo captured their discussion, the contents of those 2 min are known to them alone.

Also recognized in Armenia, named Digital Man of the Year in 2016, and invited by the President of the Republic, welcomed with great pomp and circumstance at the University and by the government, where he followed in the wake of the official host for a tree planting (alongside the previous winner,

---

[7] https://youtu.be/UmbCcUe6dZk

Steve Wozniak, Apple's co-founder)… and met with the country's start-ups. One must never forget how stubborn Louis is and that when he believes in something he follows it through to the end. Contacts were made to promote Open-Root to the Armenian government. But he discovered that the country really wanted to focus its development on networks, following Estonia's example. He was enthusiastic about the visit to the TUMO[8] school directed by Marie-Lou Papazian: a school based on direct experiments for children and young people, training an entire "digital" generation. In addition to its pedagogical performance, there is also the astonishing capacity for such a small country to make the diaspora work for its development.

During his meeting with the Prime Minister Louis introduced a very different project: instead of Open-Root, he presented RINA (Recursive InterNetwork Architecture).[9] This new internet architecture is designed to replace the old TCP/IP. Documented in 2008 by John Day, former ARPANET, RINA is now well-endowed by the European Union, which seems to have understood that sprinkling funds on numerous small projects is useless. This is finally a project that makes sense because to date no State has fully realized the importance of renewing the Internet's basic protocol or, if they have, the projects eventually peter out, as with the GENI[10] project in the United States at the end of the 1990s. Here, a small country with a formidable workforce and technical expertise could seize the opportunity to acquire skills that would soon be in high demand.

In short, a project is emerging with Armenia. It should be noted that since November 2018 the country has decided to switch its entire Internet to RINA with the **RINArmenia** project, Louis is now, of course, a member of the RINA Board.

There was equal enthusiasm in Mexico City where, 1 month after Donald Trump's election in the United States, Louis met with Mexican academics and intellectuals on his way to the 2016 IGF in Guadalajara. Travelling as always at his own expense, at the lowest possible cost, he took advantage of a stopover with friends to give a lecture at the COLMEX (Mexico City's main university). It was a great success and led to interviews and a documentary on Internet Governance in a country still reeling from the shock of the election of the new American President.

---

[8] https://tumo.org/en/

[9] http://pouzinsociety.org/

[10] YOUNG, Jeffrey R. Researchers Rebuild their Effort to Rebuild the Internet. *Chronicle of Higher Education*, 2008, vol. 54, no 45.

The idea of creating one's own domain names and owning one's own TLD was a highly attractive idea which quickly caught on. With each Open-Root display, enthusiasm and amazement were guaranteed.

A highly significant encounter was with the governor of a Russian province who stumbled upon a presentation of Open-Root at a UNESCO/IFAP seminar in Khanty-Mansiysk (Western Siberia). He immediately fell under the spell and, a few weeks after returning to Paris, Louis received a request for permission to distribute the text of his presentation throughout Russia. Receiving this official request from a continent where the language problem is crucial was a great delight. Two years later Russia announced the creation of a Cyrillic Root.

9.5   Digital Sovereignty

The notion of digital sovereignty became popular in France in the spring of 2014 with the publication of a book by Pierre Bellanger. Louis received a copy as a gift and was an immediate fan: finally, an author had put in words the defects of the Internet, and explained that while cybersecurity is about protecting data, digital sovereignty is about not being eaten alive by "friends". Louis' concern for network security was perfectly in line with the governance aspect developed in Pierre Bellanger's book, their ideas dovetail very nicely. In addition, both are formidable debaters and very good storytellers: friendship and mutual respect were immediately forged between them.

This was in 2015 and in France Louis Pouzin's recognition following the QEPrize was fading. He is someone who has no use for fads or frills when it comes to commenting on the situation of the Internet. Buzzwords such as blockchain, big data, Internet of things (IoT), cloud, Artificial Intelligence or AI do not matter to him. They are interesting, but not his focus.

It is all very well to talk about business intelligence, massive surveillance, fragility of TCP/IP, non-involvement of elected officials and governments… but again has not only made him friends.

The opportunity for a modest one-eighth-page article in the daily newspaper *Le Monde* came up. Pierre Bellanger proposed to Louis Pouzin and Chantal Lebrument to review Google's Internet root, in an article published on May 7, 2016. An indisputable fact since 2009, the Chrome browser is on Google's root. In terms of browsing, this makes no difference to the Internet user, but their data become the property of Google. It's no use refusing to be part of social media, using Chrome is enough for the data cruncher to start feeding.

For now, Chrome is based on a copy of ICANN's root (which is public) but the question remains: what will happen when the ogre opts for independence?

What insolence! To dare to question both ICANN's and Google's probity, in March 2016, was still a crime of lèse-majesté.

Louis' pet troll immediately set to work, directly with the IT department of the above-mentioned newspaper. Surrealist exchanges were held between the authors of the text and a representative of the newspaper. The professional quality of this troll being recognized… for his perfect knowledge of ICANN's RFCs,[11] Louis Pouzin was thrown to the wolves. Even the publication of a clarification text providing evidence of the reality of Google's root was not enough.

It took the support of Internet users denouncing this troll, known to all as such and already banned from several networks, for the editor to agree to not remove the article and especially to not apologize to his readers for having published false information. The troll, warm behind his keyboard in his small civil servant position, seems to have been asked not to interfere too wildly in the discussions, especially during his working hours. Or a kinder view would be that he has acknowledged his mistake. The fact remains that gagging Louis Pouzin is quite difficult. As he often says, to be recognized in France you have to be either a singer or a soccer player. Philosophical, he prefers to look to the future and above all to take pleasure in what he does. If working 16 h a day, sleeping four to 6 h and spending your holidays in low-cost planes to go to conferences is like an addiction, then yes, Louis Pouzin is a druggy, high on governance, security and the digital sovereignty of the Internet.

---

[11] RFC: https://en.wikipedia.org/wiki/Request_for_Comments

10

The New Internets (2014–Present)

10.1 Lessons from Open Roots

Louis is not particularly interested in money, even though he recognizes its usefulness—who wants to be poor? He hates the verbiage of communicators, trendy words and false issues such as net neutrality. He has only one goal: to make progress. At conferences he sees many prestigious brand companies and OIVs (Operators of Vital Importance) running their business on an unsecured internet and he tries to explain to them how having their own TLD could help parry the defects of TCP/IP, allowed them to continue to operate when the ICANN root is down or their company is the victim of a ransomware attack. In such cases, private communication within an organization through a global intranet would be an obvious competitive advantage. Useful as that is however, the main reason for an open root is that one is no longer bogged down in domain name portfolio issues: owning your TLD means that you can create as many second-level domain names as needed, freely.

Louis does not spare himself, he tirelessly shares the Open-Root Proof of Concept (PoC) to raise interest, give ideas, but these are systematically retooled as soon as the project reaches the level of network and IT managers. This is hardly surprising in France where all IT Managers have made their way in the current system and do not want to start learning new skills when they are all over 40 years old. In addition, patches and IT solutions for data security have a commercial appeal against which Open-Root cannot compete: luxurious presentation, installed and indestructible lobbies and above all, price. Indeed, telling people that domain names are fluff, without any value, and that creating or modifying a second-level domain name costs almost nothing, is not a

© Springer Nature Switzerland AG 2020
C. Lebrument, F. Soyez, *The Inventions of Louis Pouzin*,
https://doi.org/10.1007/978-3-030-34836-6_10

sales pitch, especially when the service is three or four orders of magnitude lower than what is found on the market. Prestige is also about cost, as a famous car advertisement said: "Not expensive enough, my son". Louis is no match in this game.

So, people find the idea interesting, but as an exotic invention. For a company to review its organization requires mandatory recourse to the hierarchy and, in French groups this means going through the IT Manager and if a solution is cheap, it is suspicious; if it is disruptive then it is dangerous to careers.

Louis never takes offence to these refusals.

In fact, he is so convinced that Open-Root will become a must because it is one of the only ways to guarantee Internet connection in case of an ICANN root failure or cyber-attack, that he gives himself few means to develop his concept. It is his friends and fellow enthusiasts who take action and promote technical solutions for Open-Root deployment or struggle to hold demonstrations. Louis is always willing to talk about it, present and argue about it but, always a visionary, he is convinced that the future is outside TCP/IP and he feels all the advantages of encapsulating Open-Root in the New Internets that have been emerging since 2016.

Indeed, since 2018 the New Internet initiative has become mature, whether it be the Next Generation Internet (NGI)[1] led by Monique Calisti (Switzerland) and her consortium NGI4All, or the flagship laboratory in Barcelona, i2Cat,[2] dedicated to Internet research. But although these initiatives are European, they are never French, much to Louis' despair.

10.2   RINA, the Up-coming Internet

For Louis, the future is called RINA.[3] He constantly pressures decision-makers to hold at least one information meeting, so that industry and the French political body do not once again find themselves lagging behind when RINA is finally adopted.[4]

In France, state and industrial entities are indeed interested in information on these flourishing New Internet sites, but remain unaware of the media's ignorance of the reality of the Internet, especially in the face of themes that are

---

[1] https://www.ngi.eu/

[2] http://www.i2cat.net/en

[3] Recursive InterNetwork Architecture—http://pouzinsociety.org/

[4] http://www.martingeddes.com/the-rina-revolution-is-ready-to-roll/

much more saleable and exciting such as the miracles expected from the Blockchain or the billions of dollars that will be generated by the Internet of Things… all based on a faltering Internet.

So, since 2017, Louis has been promoting RINA.

2017 was nevertheless a difficult year for him because in the spring of his 86th year Louis had difficulty getting around, everything required great effort. In the fall he had several health scares, usually just before or after a presentation since he will never change his agenda to spare himself. A cardiac alert was finally taken seriously and was resolved in a very pragmatic way by the octogenarian. A successful heart operation in January 2018 restored his health, even though he still tires quickly. Once again, he can climb stairs, walk, hike. This physical renewal that could have encouraged him to slow down and finally retire, on the contrary, gives him renewed energy to convince all and sundry that RINA is THE solution.

10.2.1 RINA: Louis' Legacy and Vision

It must be said that the belle is difficult to identify, she has too many geeks at her bedside. Reading the Wikipedia page[5] which is supposed to explain what RINA is, leads only to more confusion (no French version, only the laboratories participating in the experiment have translated it into their languages, among them Suomi). It is a big turn-off and little more has been done, even though improvements are constantly being made to the basic text.

In France, on the part of computer scientists in positions of responsibility, all in their forties, after having built their careers on their knowledge of TCP/IP, bottle-fed by Microsoft and anti-fraud patch developments, the idea of a new, simple-to-develop architecture repulses them. There is no one more hostile to the very idea of looking closely at RINA than a systems administrator… which therefore blocks any evolution in many structures in the country.

Once you have understood the general gist of RINA's philosophy, it is gripping, but it remains complicated because the reference system is still in its infancy, too immature to interest a non-IT audience, while the current Internet model seems so recent that it is still called New Technologies.

This is forgetting that TCP/IP is based on datagrams, invented in 1971 by a certain Louis Pouzin. The so-called New Technologies therefore have a much older history than their current development and they seem antediluvian to the general public with their recent adoption of the Internet (barely 20 years).

---

[5] https://en.wikipedia.org/wiki/Recursive_InterNetwork_Architecture_(RINA)

To understand RINA, it is therefore necessary to contact who has been involved in developing the system, with the teaching skills to explain its meaning and, above all, with the authority to establish the technical truth: Louis Pouzin himself.

10.2.2   Understanding RINA

How to explain this new innovative architecture, launched in 2008 by John Day at Boston University, but with knotty technical references and beyond the reach of the basic Internet user, even one who is a geek? To write this synthesis and try to take stock of the new Internet revolution that is underway, it took many interviews with Louis Pouzin to understand its full scope. While the subject is sometimes mentioned in the technical media devoted to the Internet on the other side of the Atlantic, in Europe it is still confined to research and development teams with few links to industry.

> *If TCP/IP is the piston airplane, RINA is the jet age.*
>   *At the moment, it's exotic; in 20 years, it will be ordinary*
>   Martin GEDDES[6]—24/5/2018

RINA is a software architecture applicable to any connected system: computers, Internet of Things, microchips and cell phones… any system that uses communication software to interact with other machines. The goal is to have communication principles (protocols) that are shared and can be used by all objects capable of communicating.

In the previous century it was called the telephone, a tool allowing people who speak all kinds of languages to communicate with each other, as long as they understand the other's language.

RINA's objective is to enable communication between all systems, large and small, with simple means that each system can understand.

Why is it not like that right now? Because the need isn't recognized. The people who created the Internet were happy to do complicated things because it was more interesting from a technical point of view and because they all wanted to be the one to improve the system. However, every time someone tries to improve on the existing system, it becomes more complicated and therefore systems understand each other less and less.

---

[6] http://www.martingeddes.com/the-rina-revolution-is-ready-to-roll/

10.2.3   The Internet Under TCP/IP

Why are there so many security flaws in today's Internet? This is because the definition of protocols was not designed to examine all particular cases, the variants. The worst is when these protocols evolve, and a new version simply replaces the old one.

When systems are not up to date, they use outdated variants and the Internet ends up becoming an imprecise communication system. Variants can be interpreted in different ways and one system will not share the same updated versions. What is right for one system will be wrong for another.

A system is not secure when it is able to do things that hadn't been foreseen, and when these actions are hostile or costly or ambiguous, they disrupt the normal functioning of exchanges.

The problem with the current Internet is the variants.

For the moment, variants are included in the basic implementation. It is the applications, developments or uses that induce these variants, which are sometimes so extensive they are called ecosystems. They constitute a set of existing procedures, customs, language and systems. Of course, diversity and specific conventions will always be essential, but the objective is that these variants should not prevent the construction of a universal communication system.

In today's Internet all these variants make communication complicated because not everyone has the same interpretation.

The most frequent case is that of updates, which remain a risk because not all special cases have been planned for and there are many people who are not aware of them, thus leading to communication mismatches. Inaccurate protocols lead to a certain culture of uncertainty. Hackers are very familiar with these particular cases, but this unpublished knowledge comes from people who misuse the protocols because of a lack of requirements, or from fraudsters who know about the cases of malfunctioning and use them among themselves to take advantage of incidents for their own benefit.

10.2.4   Today's Internet Soup

All systems are ultimately made up of physical elements: even if their operating algorithms have been thoroughly tested, they work in the physical world and are by definition sensitive; there may be imperfectly produced microprocessors, contacts that shouldn't be there but are, and this is inherent to any system that has physical components.

The Internet is currently too complex and impossible to secure because it is compartmentalized: not all applications can run on all machines or specialized systems. If we have the impression that everything is fine, it is because the people who make them work have years of experience, have seen numerous failures, know where the weak points are, and can quickly identify problem causes.

This is how we live with a system that is not actually very solid.

10.3   RINA According to Louis Pouzin

In today's Internet there are tens of thousands of ways to compose commands, requests or exchanges between different systems, each with its own way of expressing itself, dubbed syntax, as in human languages. In RINA the command language is realized in an unconventional way.

The syntax of German is not the same as that of English or Hindi, etc. Communication is only possible if there is a shared syntax.

The particularity of RINA is that it defines parameters and sets conditions that must be met by all systems in their communication protocol so as to be understood by all other systems. Therefore, there must be few of them and they must be simple. They must be simple enough so that everyone who installs these systems can understand them without misinterpretation.

This cannot be done through a universal protocol because this would entail as many versions as there are special cases. This is the situation with the current Internet, which is made up of a multitude of special cases.

So, by creating a basic structure in which the transmission of the interpretation of the language being used is very simple, those who understand the language can build their arguments, develop them and use them for their specific activities.

10.3.1   RINA Is Based on Recursivity

This concept is not easy to understand.

Recursivity is the ability to reuse functions (principles, regulations or software) using the same programs but with different parameters. If an algorithm is known to be correct, it means that it has always worked and that if parameters are changed it will continue to work. But the principle "*if it ain't broke, don't fix it*" is not always a good idea because nothing else must change and that is often not the case. It must be simple, easily understandable by all, well tested and made autonomous. That is why security in RINA is grounded in the simplicity of the basic techniques, on independence and also on specific development methodologies whenever additional functions are added. Indeed, when one part of the system depends on another, it remains a risk. Any dependence between systems must be limited to well-known minimum functions that do not correlate with the physics or logic of other systems. It must be possible to immediately detect where any problem comes from.

In networks, to prove that a system works, it is not enough to prove that it works when the other parts are working well, one must prove that it works when others aren't. When building increasingly complex systems, the general rule is that each piece of a complex system must be simple so that it can be proven to work well when other pieces do not.

This does not mean that it will always work well, just that it will be easy to determine what the cause of any malfunction is.

In today's Internet, due to ageing, systems are never quite what they should be.

When there is no self-control or neighborhood control system, security goes to pot: one never knows what the root of a problem is nor where to look, so fixing things can take days or even weeks, which can cause significant losses.

10.3.2 The RINA Functions

In RINA the foundations are very simple, and functions can be added for specific tasks. These functions can be modified as needed, as long as precise parameters are used. That is, every time orders, requests or answers are exchanged between two systems, the basic commands must be universal, then one can add things.

Let us take the example of a restaurant and its menu. Anyone can choose from among the dishes on the menu. The restaurant can serve very different people as long as a few basic principles are respected, such as having a menu, and listing prices and payment means. Specificities of some users are defined by referring to rules, the restaurant's menu. All this is simple, universal, shared and known by all.

This is what RINA allows: to deploy as many variants as necessary without forcing everyone to use them. Only the users or applications of these variants need to know that they exist and what can be done with them.

10.3.3   RINA's Strengths

Complexity is the main enemy of security. A system that is very simple is much safer than a system that is complicated. The more complex a system is for people (not for machines), the more likely it is that there will be safety errors.

RINA's strength lies in the simplicity of the protocols used, they can be examined thoroughly. This does not mean that there will never be any errors, just that there won't be as many and that they will be easy to fix because they will fall within specific operating frameworks.

10.3.4   Why Talk About a Bubble Internet for RINA

When you have a program that works, you would like to add additional functions. If they are already installed elsewhere, the two systems are put together, for example two RINA operations, and are linked to each other, specifying the functions that must be transferred from one to the other. At the beginning, in conferences, the term "bubbles" was used, but the term "subprogram" is more accurate.

For maintenance, the people who manage a RINA project must know the particularities of two systems, but when there are three, four, five, etc., they must also know the defects of all the others, which is not possible. In other words, when you set up a system composed of several other systems, each subprogram can be considered independent, but when they are all together it is something else, it is not just 25 subprograms together, it is a new system, that can even have other subprograms between them.

In this case, the recursive aspect of RINA means that you can add as many subprograms as you want, and each one can be contained in another or not, be next to another or contain other.

10.3.5   RINA Is Independent

Today there are a few thousand basic commands in the Internet because many of these commands are specific to certain uses. In RINA there is no need to keep pasting the same things back into the code, why should everything be present at the same time? When typing in a "copy" command, it should always work… but doesn't.

The trouble is mainly due to ignorance. People don't know what is going on so try things out to see what will happen. These particularities are not recorded in RINA, they are simply "recognizable". RINA's strength is that it can recognize them and transfer them without modifying them in any way. It simply communicates the information from one system to another and it is then up to each user system to process the parameters that concern it—or not to process them if they do not concern it—and to produce the appropriate results only for those who have requested it and who are authorized to make the request.

In other words, RINA is based on a kind of internal filtering system, whereas outside RINA there is no filter, everything goes everywhere, a command is sent, and the command parameters can be sent to anyone. If only software is involved, it causes little damage.

10.3.6 Programming in RINA

Each RINA process is designed as a piece of code in Algol[7] or Perl or some other language. There has traditionally been an intellectual separation between people who created systems and those who created languages. While early programming languages were mainly computational, Fortran for example, they have become more and more complex. The objects processed by a language can now be lists, trees, subprograms, whatever. In the case of a new language created by expanding an existing language, all kinds of technical objects can be expressed that are much more complex than adding, subtracting, etc. This means that a large number of people have not understood the difference. They think that just because a sequence of characters is called "thingy" then everything is all set. But that is not true at all. It works if it has been demonstrated that executing a piece of code that has been added has data formats and capacity limits that are tolerable and adapted to the user. But most people don't know this and don't care.

Domain names were invented by ICANN in 1998, but using a system funded by users. Just imagine the ITU[8] in Geneva offering telephone numbers, selling them and, every time someone asks for a telephone number, making them pay. This can be useful when there is a large number of requests, for example with taxes or weather forecasts, but it is not necessary for this to be managed by a single private organization.

As far as domain names are concerned, identifiers will always be needed. In a set of applications, applications or people working on the same data, must

---

[7] http://www.softwarepreservation.org/projects/ALGOL
[8] https://www.itu.int/fr/about/Pages/default.aspx

each be able to define the data on which it is working: "I am referring to this particular data set".

But one has to agree on an identification system. RINA has as many naming systems as needed because the programming has been done with tools that date back about 40 years: the Algol, designed in 1950 by John Backus and Peter Naur. However, systems people have never taken an interest in this. They consider it programming, abstraction and were never interested because it was not directly related to machines.

The authors of the Algol language had understood that an identifier was only valid for a certain part of a program and made no sense elsewhere. An identifier can be referenced externally if there is communication with another program that serves as an identifier, in which case the program's identifiers will be declared as being used by another, establishing a correlation. But this correlation is not universal, it is specific to the program coupling.

The creators of the Internet were oblivious to this language culture, for them an identifier constituted a machine address or an address in a programming language, in a piece of code….

This confusion has created a huge mess. There is no systematic identification when writing Internet programs.

Domain names were not at all designed for identification purposes, they were just meant to finance a system that only exists for those who use it. One can have specific identifiers for applications with reference systems that are already traditionally used in programming systems which are referring to another system altogether.

10.3.7 The Concept of DIF Allocator

The concept of DIF Allocator is an important component of the RINA architecture. Let's clarify a few terms.

DIF = Distributed IPC Facility

IPC = Inter Process Communication.

Scope = a part of a program or data that is visible, which is not necessarily reciprocal. To be associated with properties: read **or** write, read **and** write, accessible or not, etc. There are no standards to define the parameters of a scope.

The purpose of allocating DIFs is to manage the links between processes. It is an "inter process communication" (IPC) between various processes that may have different scopes.

The current Internet is weak precisely because it does not know the notion of scope which part of the Algol language is.

During the process of requesting the allocation of IPC resources by an application, it is up to the DIF Allocator to determine to which distributed inter-process function the allocation should be delivered. If the resource is available on a DIF that is not visible or accessible, the DIF allocator will set up an IPC process to join the DIF, or it will cooperate with other DIF allocators to create a DIF with sufficient scope to enable an IPC.

If Louis Pouzin is so involved in this new Internet it is because, without fuss but with a nicely consistent approach, RINA developments are multiplying and are starting to gain in visibility.

There are operational test benches and traffic test generators, developer hackathons and industrial applications. RINA is made up of ongoing projects[9] monitored by teams from research and industry: IRATI, ARCFIRE, OCARINA, rLITE, RINAsim, PRISTINE Project, etc.

At the last RINA general assembly in the spring of 2018, the list[10] of companies and research centers represented—Ericsson, Ciena,[11] Telefonica, Vodafone—shows that RINA is no longer a project but a new revolution that is leading to paradigm changes in how we think about the Internet. The implementation of key technologies such as the blockchain Cardano[12] or CIENA[13] Cloud computing or the VANET[14] system for intelligent cars are based on RINA protocols.

This led Martin Geddes to write in an article on RINA that it is the "killer distributed app" and that the RINA revolution is on its way[15]… but since it is an architecture and not a protocol, its implementation will be carried out transparently in all layers of society in the months and years to come.

On the cusp of his eighty-eighth birthday, Louis Pouzin has thus found yet another exciting technological revolution in which to invest all his fame and energy.

He remains at the forefront of technical developments on the Internet, always with a view to better shared and distributed governance, which respects the particularities of each people.

---

[9] http://pouzinsociety.org/research/projects

[10] http://ict-arcfire.eu/index.php/2018/06/10/rina-workshop-2018-report/

[11] https://www.encqor.ca/

[12] http://pouzinsociety.org/node/53

[13] https://www.encqor.ca/

[14] http://ict-arcfire.eu/wp-content/uploads/2018/06/VANET-RINA-1.0-1.pdf

[15] RINA Team publications: http://csr.bu.edu/rina/documents2.html

11

Epilogue

Yes, France is a nation of inventors, it is recognized as a center of excellence which has provided the world with some of the greatest scientists over the centuries.

Who invented the brilliant principle of "swiping" the iPhone screen: Jean-Marie Hullot, a Frenchman, who preferred his private life to expatriation in Silicon Valley. And in 1973, the first microcomputer, the Micral N, was invented by François Gernelle. Swallowed by Bull, this French invention was quickly scrapped in favor of a less efficient in-house product. Sounds familiar somehow… Is ignoring inventors a French specialty?

In such a context, how do you write a biography of Louis Pouzin? A man who certainly designed the Internet but also invented the Shell script, now universally used, who fought IBM's omnipotence in the 1960s and has opposed Internet monopolies since the 2000s. Always at cross purposes.

Yes, it is difficult to grasp such a man… who is nevertheless disconcertingly humble and simple. Louis Pouzin is always looking to the future and resists positive speak and the social hype around buzz words such as Blockchain, IoT, AI, Cloud, etc.

Thinking for the long term, imagining the future without being influenced by flashy trends, analyzing and documenting matters thoroughly before sharing his reflections is who Louis Pouzin is.

He is a scientific researcher whose motto is to never judge a book by its cover. He is a visionary whose predictions have often proved true even though proffered without diplomacy.

© Springer Nature Switzerland AG 2020
C. Lebrument, F. Soyez, *The Inventions of Louis Pouzin*,
https://doi.org/10.1007/978-3-030-34836-6_11

Because another of his character traits is to always say what he thinks outright, without beating about the bush, no matter how much his ideas may shock. For him, only the effectiveness and purpose of actions count.

As he loves to repeat, "if you don't have any enemies, it's because you aren't doing anything interesting".

Because this man who imagined the technical protocol of what has become the Internet, is also a hard worker, a leader, a talent scout. He had the intelligence to identify, hire and create a group of researchers who led a true crusade against the establishment with Cyclades, their industrial successes killed in the bud by a newly elected government under the sway of vested interests.

The "Cyclamen" fought a battle that proved to be the nexus of French excellence, recognized worldwide. Louis Pouzin has spanned two centuries with analyses and character intact, sometimes at the cost of angering colleagues who have not had to endure the vicissitudes that Louis has known over the course of his career.

Although Louis traced his path in the twentieth and twenty-first centuries, it was a struggle, without any gratitude from the authorities in his own country. He has however been justly recognized elsewhere: he has been received three times by Her Majesty Queen Elizabeth II for his engineering accomplishments. The French establishment which has always criticized him and put him down finally began to realize, in 2013, what an essential role this little Frenchie played in the design of the invention that revolutionized our lives: the Internet.

Louis continues to innovate, he is now working on a revolutionary new vision of the Internet with an alternative to TCP/IP: RINA. For him, the current Internet under TCP/IP is now obsolete, in 10 years its place will be in a museum. The future is RINA and its architecture based on reliable computing that is not subject to the stranglehold and the force of the lobbies. A network where developments do not require impossible to manage updates. RINA's recursiveness, speed and bandwidth gain will support the development of an Internet that truly meets the world's expectations.

An original thinker, a voice that never fears to speak the uncomfortable truths about the realities. An octogenarian, tired but still just as determined to move forward as ever, he willingly shares his knowledge to further understanding of new areas of research. His life is a Chinese shadow puppet show of the birth of the technologies that make up our daily lives.

This book is therefore also the means to set the record straight: the invention of the Internet is as much a European saga as it is an American one.

Bibliography

1962

CORBATÓ, Fernando J, MERWIN-DAGGETT, Marjorie, DALEY, Robert C. – *An experimental time-sharing system*, Spring Joint Computer, AFIPS Conference Proceedings, 1962. http://larch-www.lcs.mit.edu:8001/~corbato/sjcc62/

1967

ARPA, Advanced Research Projects Agency – Project MAC Progress Report, Volume 4, Massachusetts Institute of Technology, July 1967. http://www.dtic.mil/dtic/tr/fulltext/u2/681342.pdf

1970

POUZIN, Louis – *Le système METEOS*. « l'Informatique » magazine, July 1970a, n°6, pp 46-54
POUZIN, Louis – *Multi-processor problems and tools for process coordination*. NATO International, Summer School, Copenhagen (Denmark), Aug. 1970b, 30 p.

© Springer Nature Switzerland AG 2020
C. Lebrument, F. Soyez, *The Inventions of Louis Pouzin*,
https://doi.org/10.1007/978-3-030-34836-6

1972

POUZIN, Louis – *Rapport d'analyse du projet Cyclades*. Institut de Recherche d'Informatique et d'Automatique (IRIA), cotation GAL 510, June 1972a, 2 vol., 250 p.
The main document contains the organization, expectations and costs of the Cyclades project

1973

POUZIN, Louis – *Network design philosophies*. INFOTECH n°24, Network systems and software, London (UK), Febr. 1973a, pp 134-156.
POUZIN, Louis – *Network architectures and components*. 1st European Workshop on Computer Networks, Arles (Fr), Apr. 1973b, 35 p.
POUZIN, Louis – *Efficiency of full-duplex synchronous data link procedures*. IFIP WG6.1, INWG #35, June 1973c, 9 p.
Proceedings of the June 7–10, 1976, national computer conference, San Diego (USA), ACM, 1976, pp 571-576.
POUZIN, Louis – *Network protocols*. NATO International advanced study institute on computer communication networks, University of Sussex, Brighton (UK), Sept.1973d, pp 231-255.
GRANGÉ, J., POUZIN, L. – *Cigale, la machine de commutation de paquets du réseau Cyclades*. Congrès AFCET, Rennes, Nov. 1973, pp 249-263.
POUZIN, Louis – *Interconnection of packet switching networks*. IFIP/WG 6.1, INWG #42, NIC 20792, Oct. 1973, 19 p. http://iuwg.net/images/Pouzin-1973.pdf
POUZIN, Louis – *Presentation and major design aspects of the CYCLADES computer network*. Proceedings of the third ACM symposium on Data communications and Data networks, St Petersburg, Florida (USA), Nov.1973e, pp 80-87.
ZIMMERMANN, Hubert – *Vers une formalisation des protocoles dans un réseau d'ordinateurs. Application au réseau CYCLADES*. AFCET Congress, Rennes (Fr), Nov. 1973, pp 277-291.

1974

POUZIN, L., ZIMMERMANN, H. *Présentation du Réseau Cyclades. Introduction générale aux réseaux et à Cyclades*. Institut de Recherche d'Informatique et d'Automatique (IRIA), Febr. 1974, 10 p.
POUZIN, Louis – *A proposal for interconnecting packet switching Networks*. INWG #60, Brunel University (UK), May 1974a, pp. 1023-1036. https://www.dropbox.com/s/sjfoa7op8iu9xc3/INWG-60_Pouzin_optimized.pdf

CERF, Vinton, KAHN, Robert. *A Protocol for Packet Network Intercommunication,* IEEE, Vol Com-22, May 5 1974. http://www.cs.princeton.edu/courses/archive/fall06/cos561/papers/cerf74.pdf

POUZIN, Louis – *CIGALE, the packet switching machine of the CYCLADES computer network.* IFIP Stockholm (Sw.), Aug.1974b, p. 155-159. http://www.rogerdmoore.ca/PS/CIGALE/CIGALE.html

POUZIN, Louis – *The Economics of computer networks. The Cyclades cases.* International Symposium on Economics of informatics, Mayence (All.), Sept. 1974c, vol. 2, p. 79-88.

POUZIN, Louis – *Le réseau Cyclades.* Revue Technique Française n°2, avril 1974, 4 p. Included in *l'Informatique* on March 1975a, p. 12-15.

FARZA M.N., SERGEANT G. – *Machine interprétative pour la mise en œuvre d'un langage de commande sur le Réseau Cyclades.* PhD Thesis presented at the Faculty of Sciences of the University of Toulouse, Oct. 1974, 231 p.

POUZIN, Louis – *Informatique et télécommunications.* « Avenirs » magazine, ONISEP, n°258, Nov. 1974d, p. 23-25.

POUZIN, Louis – *Structure d'une procédure de transmission point-à-point.* Institut de Recherche d'Informatique et d'Automatique (IRIA), Dec. 1974e, 11 p.

1975

ZIMMERMANN, Hubert – *Terminal access in the CYCLADES computer network.* ICS 75, Juan les Pins (Fr), June 1975, p. 97-99.

POUZIN, Louis – *Une méthode pour la normalisation des réseaux de commutation de paquets.* Institut de Recherche d'Informatique et d'Automatique (IRIA), Jan. 1975b, 12 p.

POUZIN, Louis – *Basic elements of a network data link control procedure (NDLC).* ACM SIGCOMM Computer Communication Review, Jan. 1975c, vol. 5, n°1, p. 6-23.

IRLAND, Marek – *Simulation of CIGALE, Report on assumptions and results.* University of Waterloo (Ca.), Jan.1975a, 54 p.

BREMER, J., DANTHINE, A. – *Communication protocols in a network context.* ACM SIGCOMM-SIGOPS, Santa Monica (USA), March 1975, 6 p.

CERF V. , CURRAN A. – *The work of IFIP working Group 6.1.* ACM SIGCOMM, Computer Communication Review, April 75 1974, vol.5, n°2, p. 18-27. Chairman: Louis Pouzin.

POUZIN, Louis – *Logique d'adaptation à un réseau de commutation de paquets.* Institut de Recherche d'Informatique et d'Automatique (IRIA), April 1975d, 26 p.

DANTHINE A., ESCHENAUER E. – *Simulation de procédures de transmission dans CIGALE.* Liège University (Bel.), 1975, 17p.

ELIE, M., ZIMMERMANN, H. – *Transport protocol. Standard end-to-end protocol for heterogeneous computer networks.* IFIP WG6.1, INWG#61, May 1975, 33 p.

POUZIN, Louis – *An integrated approach to network protocols.* Proceedings, national computer conference and exposition, ACM, May 1975e, p. 701-707. https://www.computer.org/csdl/proceedings/afips/1975/5083/00/50830701.pdf

WOOD, David C. – *A survey of the capabilities of 8 packet switching networks.* Institute of Electrical and Electronic Engineers (IEEE) Computer Society; US National Bureau of Standards, 1975, p. 1-7.

POUZIN, Louis – *The CYCLADES Network, Present state and developments trends.* IEEE Symposium, Gaithersburg (USA), June 75, p. 8-13.

IRLAND, Marek – *Simulation of CIGALE 1975b, Progress Report: phase I – simulation for the period from April to June 30, 75.* University of Waterloo (Ca.), July 1975, 27 p.

POUZIN, Louis – *Congestion control based on channel load.* Institut de Recherche d'Informatique et d'Automatique (IRIA), Aug. 1975f, 5 p.

GRANGÉ J.L., JASTRABSKY N. – *Exploitation du réseau Cigale*, Computer Meeting, Sept.1975, 19 p.

POUZIN, Louis – *Standards in data communications and computer networks.* Fourth Data Communications Symposiums, Québec City (Ca.), Oct. 1975g, 2.8-2.12.

NAFFAH, Najah – *Présentation du système TIPAC.* Institut de Recherche d'Informatique et d'Automatique (IRIA), nov. 1975a, 15 p.

POUZIN, Louis – *Les réseaux. Concepts et structures, tutoriel.* INFOREP, St Maximin (Fr), Dec. 1975h, 101 p.

NAFFAH, Najah – *Étude de la gestion des terminaux dans un réseau général informatique et développement d'un système microprogrammé pour la connexion directe d'un terminal intelligent sur le Réseau CYCLADES.* PhD thesis in engineering, University Paris VI – (Fr), Dec. 1975b, 237 p.

POUZIN, Louis – *Computer Communication Networks.* NATO advanced Study Intitutes series, edited by R.L. Grimsdale (Univ. of Sussex, UK) and F.F.Kuo (Univ. Hawaii, USA), Nordhoff-Leyden, 1975i, 255 p.

1976

POUZIN, Louis – *The CYCLADES Network - Present state and development trends.* Instytut Doskonalenia Kadr Kierowniczych Administracji Pal̆ stwowej (Pol.), 1976a.

POUZIN, Louis – *Virtual circuits vs. datagrams: technical and political problems.* AFIPS, Proceedings National Computer Conference, ACM, June 1976b, p. 483-494.

POUZIN, Louis – *Distributed congestion control in a packet network: The channel load limiter.* GI-6. Jahrestagung. Springer, Berlin, Heidelberg (All.), 1976c. p. 16-21.

POUZIN, Louis – *Names and objects in heterogeneous computer networks*. Conference of the European Cooperation in Informatics. Springer, Berlin, Heidelberg, (All.), 1976d. p. 1-11.

NAFFAH, N. – *Implementation of host protocols in an intelligent terminal connected to the CYCLADES computer network*. MIMI 76, Zurich (Swiss), June 1976a, 4 p.

POUZIN, Louis – *The network business, Monopolies and entrepreneurs*. ICCC 76, Toronto (Ca.), Aug. 1976e, p. 563-567

POUZIN, Louis – *Flow control in data networks. Methods and tools*. ICCC 76, Toronto (Ca.), Aug. 1976f, P. 467-474.

POUZIN, Louis – *Distributed computer systems*. 1976g. http://cds.cern.ch/record/866857/files/p23.pdf

LE BIHAN, Jean – *Manuel de raccordement d'équipements informatiques au Réseau Cyclades*. Institut de Recherche d'Informatique et d'Automatique (IRIA), Febr. 1976, 14 p.

GRANGÉ, Jean-Louis – *CIGALE, the packet switching subnetwork of CYCLADES*. Medical IT Days, Toulouse, (Fr.) March 1976a, 9 p.

POUZIN, Louis – *The case for a revision of X 25*. ACM SIGCOMM Computer Communication Review, July 1976h, vol. 6, n°3, p. 17-20.

POUZIN, Louis – *Distributed congestion control in a packet network: the channel load limiter*. 6th Congress Gesellschaft für Informatik, Stuttgart (All.), Sept. 76, p. 16-21.

NAFFAH, Najah – *Multiplexeur Microprogrammé de Liaisons Virtuelles (MLV)*. Institut de Recherche d'Informatique et d'Automatique (IRIA), Nov. 1976b, 23 p.

GRANGÉ, Jean-Louis – *L'expérience d'un réseau de commutation de paquets : CIGALE, de la conception à l'exploitation*. AFCET, Gif-sur-Yvette (Fr.), Nov. 1976b, 10 p.

FOURNIER, Robert – *Le traitement par lots dans un réseau hétérogène, implémentation du serveur OS/MVT sur « IBM 360/67 » pour le Réseau CYCLADES*. PhD, Grenoble University – Dec. 1976, 167 p. https://tel.archives-ouvertes.fr/tel-00010533/document

QUINT, *Vincent – Protection logicielle contre les erreurs dans un réseau d'ordinateurs hétérogène - Application à l'IBM 360/67 du réseau CYCLADES*. PhD, Grenoble University, Dec. 1976, 129 p. https://tel.archives-ouvertes.fr/tel-00010534/document

1977

POUZIN, Louis – *A restructuring of X25 into HDLC*. ACM SIGCOMM Computer Communication Review, Jan. 1977a, vol. 7, n°1, p. 9-28.

EYRIES F., GIEN M. – *Online performance measurement in the Cyclades computer network*. EUROCON Venice (Ital.), January 77 1977, 6 p.

WEBER, S. – *Concentrateur Cyclades, manuel de référence*, Institut de Recherche d'Informatique et d'Automatique (IRIA), April 1977a, 30 p.

WEBER, S. – *Concentrateur Cyclades, introduction aux concepts et à l'usage*, Institut de Recherche d'Informatique et d'Automatique (IRIA), May 1977b, 52 p.

GRANGÉ, Jean-Louis – *Operating the CIGALE packet switching network: concepts, techniques and results.* European Conference on Electronics, EUROCON 77, Venice (Ital.), May 1977, p. 3.1.6.1- 3.1.6.6.

DANG QUOC Ky – *Cyclades in 77 : organisation, tools and services*, Institut de Recherche d'Informatique et d'Automatique (IRIA), June 1977, 9 p.

GRANGÉ, J.L., ZIMMERMANN, H. – *Les réseaux à commutation de paquets principes et exemples.* Symposium Rennes (Fr.), Juin 1977, p. 13

POUZIN, Louis – *Existing and futurs networks.* Institut de Recherche d'Informatique et d'Automatique (IRIA), july 1977b, 18 p.

ZIMMERMANN, Hubert – *The CYCLADES experience – Results and Impacts.* IFIP 77, Toronto (Ca.), Aug. 1977, 5 p.

POUZIN, Louis – *Packet Networks – Issues and choices.* IFIP 77, Toronto (Ca.), Aug. 1977c, p. 515-521.

ZIMMERMANN, H., NAFFAH, N. – *On open systems architecture.* ICCC 78, Kyoto (Jap.), Nov. 1977, 19 p.

1978

GRANGÉ J.L., MUSSARD P. – *Performance measurements of line control protocols in the CIGALE Network*, Symposium Liège (Belg.), Febr. 1978, pp. G2-1/G2-13.

POUZIN, L, ZIMMERMANN, H. – *A tutorial on protocols.* Proceedings of the IEEE, 1978, vol. 66, n°11, p. 1346-1370.

IRLAND, Marek – *Buffer management in a packet switch.* IEEE transactions on Communications, 1978, vol. 26, n°3, p. 328-337. https://pdfs.semanticscholar.org/5331/a99b793e140c8e3d1962abd4db7f86f0cd5c.pdf

EYRIES F., PUJOLLE G. – *Validation et prediction of performance in the CIGALE network.* IRIA Laboria, May 1978, 13 p.

CERF Vinton – *The Catenet Model for InternetWorking.* DARPA/IPTO IEN #48, July 1978. www.rfc-editor.org/ien/ien48.txt

NAFFAH, N., Zimmermann, H. – *Protocol converters and user interface in the CYCLADES Network.* 3rd Berkeley Workshop on Distributed Data Management and Computer Networks, Berkeley (USA), Aug. 1978, 27 p.

1979

GRANGÉ, Jean-Louis – *Operation of the Cyclades Network*. Interlinking of Computer Networks. Springer, Dordrecht (All.), 1979. p. 411-419.

DENIS, J-J, GIBERGUES, O, DE COURTABOEUF, GIXI ZA – *Principes de conversion entre les protocoles Cyclades et X25*. Proceedings of the International Symposium on Flow Control in Computer Networks, Versailles (Fr.), Febr. 1979, p. 379.

1981

POUZIN, Louis – *Methods, tools, and observations on flow control in packet-switched data networks*. IEEE Transactions on Communications, 1981, vol. 29, n°4, p. 413-426.

1992

LEE, John A.N., ROSIN Robert – *The Project MAC Interviews*, IEEE Annals of the History of Computing, 1992

1995

HUITEMA, Christian – *Et Dieu créa l'Internet*, Eyrolles, 1995.

1998

MAURIAC, Laurent, PEYRET, Emmanuèle – « *Et la France ne créa pas l'internet…* ». Libération newspaper, 27/3/1998a.

MAURIAC, Laurent, PEYRET, Emmanuèle – *Profile : « Pouzin, inventeur de génie »*. Libération, 27/3/1998b.

GRISET, Pascal – *Informatique, politique industrielle, Europe: entre plan calcul et unidata*. 1998, Institut d'histoire de l'industrie, Rive Droite (Fr.).

1999

ABBATE, Janet. – *Inventing the Internet*, MIT Press,1999, Cambridge and London.

2000

POUZIN, Louis – *The Origin of the Shell*, 2000a. www.multicians.org/shell.html
POUZIN, Louis – *Cyclades ou comment perdre un marché*. La Recherche, 2000b, n°328, p. 32-33.

2002

POUZIN, Louis – *Le projet Cyclades (1972b-1977)*. Entreprises et histoire, 2002, n°1, p. 33-40.
ATTEN, M., HENRY, P., ZIMMERMANN, H. – *La demande en réseau de transmission de données et/ou en réseau inter-ordinateurs*. Entreprises et histoire, 2002, n°1, p. 61-66.
ATTEN, Michel – *Informatique et télécommunications, une première confrontation*. Entreprises et histoire, 2002, n°1, p. 21-32.

2004

HAUBEN, R., CERF, V. – *The Internet : On its International Origins and Collaborative Vision (A Work In Progress)*. Amateur Computerist, 2004, vol. 12, n° 2, p. 5-28. www.columbia.edu/~rh120/other/misc/haubenpap.rtf

2005

WIDROW, Bernard, HARTENSTEIN Reiner, HECHT-NIELSEN Robert – *Eulogy*, IEEE Computational Intelligence Society, août 2005, http://helios.informatik.uni-kl.de/euology.pdf

2007

BELTRAN, A., GRISET, P. – *Histoire d'un pionnier de l'informatique : 40 ans de recherche à l'INRIA*, EDP Sciences, 2007.
SCHAFER, Valérie – *Le réseau Cyclades et Internet : quelles opportunités pour la France des années 1970 ?* Séminaire Haute technologie, March 14, 2007a. https://www.economie.gouv.fr/files/schafer-reseau-cyclades.pdf

SCHAFER, Valérie – *Circuits virtuels et datagrammes : une concurrence à plusieurs échelles*. Histoire, économie & société, 2007b, vol. 26, n° 2, p. 29-48. https:// www.cairn.info/revue-histoire-economie-et-societe-2007-2-page-29.htm

BELLIN, Isabelle – *Louis Pouzin, la tête dans les réseaux*. Interstices, 2007. https:// interstices.info/louis-pouzin-la-tete-dans-les-reseaux/

2008

MURRAY, Andrew – *Symbiotic regulation*. J. Marshall J. Computer & Info. L., 2008, vol. 26, p. 207.

2009

SCHAFER, Valérie – *L'Europe des réseaux dans les années 1970, entre coopérations et rivalités*. Interstices, 2009.

2010

MOUNIER-KUHN, Pierre-Éric – *L'informatique en France de la seconde Guerre Mondiale au Plan Calcul. L'émergence d'une science*. Paris, Presses de l'Université Paris-Sorbonne, 2010.

2011

NAFFAH, N., ZIMMERMANN, H. – *Protocol converters and user interface in the CYCLADES network*. Proceedings of the third Berkeley Workshop on distributed data management. 2011. p. 36. https://escholarship.org/content/qt8955f4zh/ qt8955f4zh.pdf#page=44

TROUVA, E., GRASA, E., DAY, J. – *Is the Internet an unfinished demo? Meet RINA!* TERENA Networking Conference (Spain), 2011, 12 p. https://pdfs.semantic-scholar.org/c339/e4db226ffb04a6386fd435608340efef1b33.pdf

2012

RUSSEL, Andrew L. – *Oral history interview with Louis Pouzin*, 2 April 2012, Charles Babbage Institute, Center for the History of Information Technology University of Minnesota. http://hdl.handle.net/11299/155666

GRANGÉ, Jean-Louis – *Oral History* interview with Jean-Louis Grangé by Andrew L. Russell, 2012.

SCHAFER, Valérie – *La France en réseaux*, CIGREF, 2012. Collection Économie et prospective numériques, ISSN 2111-6814

POUZIN, Louis – *The Origin of the Shell*. Multicians Retrieved, 2012, p. 08-14. https://multicians.org/shell.html

MASSIT-FOLLÉA, Françoise – *La gouvernance de l'Internet. Une internationalisation inachevée*. Le Temps des médias, 2012, n°1, p. 29-40.

2013

METZ, Cade – "*Say **Bonjour** to the internet's Long-Lost French Uncle*", Wired, 3/1/2013. https://www.wired.com/2013/01/louis-pouzin-internet-hall/

Queen Elizabeth Prize for Engineering – March 2013, London. http://qeprize.org/winners-2013/louis-pouzin/

MADELAINE, N. – « *Louis Pouzin : L'Internet doit être refait de fond en comble* », Les Échos, n° 21442, May 24, 2013, p. 23.

ALBERT, Éric – « *Louis Pouzin, pionnier de l'internet* ». Le Monde July, 3th July 2013, p.7.

2014

RUSSELL, A., SCHAFER, V. – *In the Shadow of ARPANET and Internet: Louis Pouzin and the Cyclades Network in the 1970s*. Technology and Culture, 2014, vol. 55, n°4, p. 880-907.

CHICHE Nathalie – *Internet : Pour une gouvernance ouverte et équitable*, 2014, Rapport du Conseil Économique, Social et Environnemental (CESE). https://www.lecese.fr/travaux-publies/internet-pour-une-gouvernance-ouverte-et-equitable

2015

MARTINICA, C., SHAPIRO, M. – *Du datagramme à la gouvernance de l'internet*, 1024 - Newsletter of the French IT Company. July 2015. https://www.societe-informatique-de-france.fr/wp-content/uploads/2015/07/1024-no6-pouzin.pdf

ARPAGIAN, Nicolas – *Définition et historique de la cybersécurité*. Collection Que Sais-Je? - 2015, vol. 2, p. 7-30.

SCHAFER, Valérie – *Part of a whole: RENATER, a twenty-year-old network within the Internet*. Information & Culture, 2015, vol. 50, n°2, p. 217-235.

2016

POUZIN, Louis – *Net Neutrality and Quality of Service*. Net Neutrality Compendium. Springer, Cham, 2016. p. 73-78.

2017

BAUMARD, Philippe – *A Brief History of Hacking and Cyberdefense. Cybersecurity in France*. Springer, Cham, 2017. p. 17-30.

RUSSELL, Andrew L. – *Hagiography, revisionism & blasphemy in Internet histories*. Internet Histories, 2017, vol. 1, n°1-2, p. 15-25.

THIERRY, BENJAMIN G., SCHAFER, V. – *From the Minitel to the Internet: The Path to Digital Literacy and Network Culture in France (1980s–1990s)*. "The Routledge Companion to Global Internet Histories". Routledge, 2017. p. 99-111.

MAILLAND, Julien – *Minitel, the Open Network Before the Internet*. The Atlantic, June 16, 2017. https://www.theatlantic.com/technology/archive/2017/06/minitel/530646/

MAILLAND, J., DRISCOLL, K. – *Minitel: Welcome to the Internet*, MIT Press, 2017. https://mitpress.mit.edu/books/minitel

2019

PALOQUE-BERGÈS, C., SCHAFER, V. *French memories about the ARPANET: a conversation with Michel Élie and Gérard Le Lann*. Internet Histories, 2019. 3(1), pp. 81-97.

COLOMBAIN, Jérôme – *Nouveau Monde*, interview Louis Pouzin, France Info, March 16, 2019. Paris (Fr.) https://www.francetvinfo.fr/replay-radio/nouveau-monde/nouveau-monde-il-faut-un-nouvel-internet-selon-louis-pouzin-lun-des-peres-du-reseau-mondial_3214327.html

CHM, Computer History Museum —*Welcomes New Fellows*, May 2019, Mountain View, CA. https://www.i-programmer.info/news/82-heritage/12743-four-fellows. html

Printed in the United States
By Bookmasters